The use and impact of dispersal orders

The use and impact of dispersal orders

Sticking plasters and wake-up calls

Adam Crawford and Stuart Lister

First published in Great Britain in 2007 by

The Policy Press
Fourth Floor, Beacon House
Queen's Road
Bristol BS8 1QU
UK

Tel no   +44 (0)117 331 4054
Fax no   +44 (0)117 331 4093
Email   tpp-info@bristol.ac.uk
www.policypress.org.uk

Published for the Joseph Rowntree Foundation by The Policy Press

ISBN 978 1 84742 078 7

British Library Cataloguing in Publication Data
A catalogue record for this book is available from the British Library.

Library of Congress Cataloging-in-Publication Data
A catalog record for this book has been requested.

Adam Crawford is Professor of Criminology and Criminal Justice and Director of the Centre for Criminal Justice Studies at the University of Leeds. **Stuart Lister** is a lecturer in criminal justice in the Law School at the University of Leeds.

The **Joseph Rowntree Foundation** has supported this project as part of its programme of research and innovative development projects, which it hopes will be of value to policy makers, practitioners and service users. The facts presented and views expressed in this report are, however, those of the authors and not necessarily those of the Foundation.

Cover image: courtesy of stock.xchng®
Cover design by Qube Design Associates, Bristol
Printed in Great Britain by Latimer Trend, Plymouth

Contents

List of figures and tables   vii
Acknowledgements   viii
Summary   ix

1   Introduction   1

2   Dispersal order powers and research overview   4
Research overview   7
Research methods   8

3   National overview   9
England and Wales   9
Scotland   10
London   11
Lessons from practice   13
Authorisation   15
Communication challenges   18
Impact on police resources   19
Implementation strategies   20
Use of escort powers   23
Exit strategies   23
Renewal   24

4   A tale of two cities   26
The use of dispersal orders in Sheffield   26
Authorisation process   27
Implementation   27
Measuring success   29
The Leeds experience   30
Impact over time   34
Conflict with youth   36

5   Two case studies   38
Wider developments   40
Police implementation   42
Impact on perceptions of residents   45
Impact on crime and ASB   46
Crime displacement   49
Young people and adult residents' surveys   53
Young people dispersed   58
Assessments by professionals   59

6   Policing and young people   **62**

Discretionary policing and summary powers   63
Policing and procedural justice   63
Relations between police and young people   65
Communicative properties   67
Young people and public space   69
Young people and risk   72

7   Conclusions and policy implications   **73**

References   **76**

List of figures and tables

Figures

1	British Crime Survey (BCS) trends in crime and perception of ASB	2
2	Number of dispersal orders in England and Wales (April–March), by year	9
3	Number of dispersal orders in Scotland, by year	10
4	Duration of dispersal orders in London 2006/07 in weeks	12
5	Type of location	12
6	Reasons given for designation	13
7	Authorisation process	16
8	Number of dispersal orders across Sheffield, by year	26
9	Number of dispersal orders across Leeds, by year	30
10	Duration of dispersal orders across Leeds (2004-06)	30
11	Number of patrol hours	43
12	Police activity data for Northston	43
13	Residents' views on effectiveness of dispersal order on crime and ASB (% at least 'slightly effective')	46
14	Residents' views of effectiveness on wider benefits (% at least 'slightly effective')	46
15	Recorded crime in Northston	47
16	Types of crime in Northston	47
17	Reports of ASB in Northston (2004-07)	48
18	Recorded crime in neighbouring dispersal zone	48
19	Types of crime in neighbouring dispersal zone	49
20	Crime in identified displacement area	50
21	Reports of ASB in identified displacement area (2004-07)	50
22	Recorded crime, Southby	51
23	Number of calls to the police, Southby	52
24	Young people's perceptions of safety	53
25	Levels of understanding about the dispersal powers	54
26	Levels of understanding about the dispersal order boundaries	55
27	Changing perceptions of Northston residents (2001/07)	55
28	Residents' views (% 'agreed')	56
29	Impact of dispersal order on young people (% 'agreed')	57
30	Young people's views (% 'agreed')	57
31	Impact of dispersal order on youths' feelings towards local police	58
32	Impact of dispersal order on youths in Northston and Southby	59

Tables

1	England and Wales, and Scotland compared	6
2	Operation Mischief (Sheffield) police performance data (2005-06)	28
3	Composition of the case study locations	39
4	Timeline of case studies	41
5	Victim of ASB in the previous 12 months	54
6	Knowledge of the dispersal order	54
7	Area has become safer/less safe as a result of the dispersal order	56

Acknowledgements

We would like to thank Christopher Carney for his considerable research assistance throughout this project. Nicola O'Leary and Jon Burnett provided valuable help in the collation of the data for which we are grateful. We would like to thank all the people who gave up their time to talk to us and those who provided us with information and insights. They are too numerous to mention by name but this research relied on their openness and generosity. In particular, we owe considerable thanks to the police and other professionals in the two case study areas, as well as to all the young people and adult residents who responded to the surveys or allowed us to interview them. We are grateful to Anna Barker and Susan Flint for reading and commenting on the final draft. Finally, thanks are due to Alison Jarvis who has patiently overseen the research, providing support and guidance throughout.

Summary

There has been considerable local variation in the take-up and use of dispersal powers. This is not linked directly to differences in the extent or type of behaviour leading to designation, but appears to be due to local preferences for particular approaches to enforcement, the willingness of key individuals to experiment with new tools and the capacity of local interests to organise and promote a police-led response.

Dispersal orders have been used in a wide range of areas to address a diversity of social problems, but are most commonly used in relation to perceived problems with groups of young people. Where anti-social behaviour (ASB) is a significant and persistent problem, dispersal orders can provide a brief period of respite and open a window of opportunity in which to develop wide-ranging preventive approaches.

Dispersal order authorisation triggers exceptional and extensive powers, with significant implications for individual freedoms. Prior designation, where informed by rigorous information collation and conducted thoroughly through stakeholder engagement and consultation, helps ensure that these powers are an appropriate, proportionate and planned response to repeated problems within a given locality.

The authorisation process is a crucial element on which well-considered dispersal orders are founded, as it affords the opportunity to enhance police–community relations and provide openness and accountability. It can serve to:

- allow examination of the evidence and consideration of proportionate responses and alternative strategies;
- stimulate multi-agency problem-solving, triggering wider and longer-term preventive and diversionary strategies; and
- foster community consultation and dialogue about appropriate use of public space and the role of community in supporting social cohesion and tolerance.

Many of the benefits that derive from dispersal orders stem from the process of authorisation and the associated activities that are triggered, rather than the powers per se.

Evidence suggests that many police and local authorities used dispersal order powers both sparingly and in ways that often sought to engage communities, including young people, in a dialogue about the parameters of acceptable behaviour, community relations and the use of public spaces.

Most frontline police welcomed the additional flexibility that dispersal powers conferred on them, particularly at a time when many felt, more generally, that their scope for discretion was being curtailed in other areas of police work. It provided them with formal authority to do what many considered to be a key aspect of traditional policing, namely engaging with groups of young people and negotiating order.

However, the discretionary and subjective nature of the powers place significant pressures of professional judgement on individual police in situations that may precipitate rather than reduce conflict. Where targeted at groups of youths, dispersal orders have the capacity to antagonise and alienate young people who frequently feel unfairly stigmatised for being in public places in the company of friends.

The enforcement of dispersal orders has significant implications for police resources as they demand heightened visible patrols and can raise false public expectations about longer-term police priorities.

In many localities, dispersal orders generated short-term displacement effects, shifting problems to other places, sometimes merely for the duration of the order. As a stand-alone response, dispersal orders constitute a 'sticking plaster' that provides a degree of immediate and localised respite but invariably fails to address the wider causes of the identified problems.

The case studies in the present study revealed:

- There was a decline in the number of young people congregating in the dispersal zones during the authorisation period. Some adult residents reported feeling more confident about going out in the area.
- Despite the police seeking to make it clear that the dispersal order did not 'ban groups from gathering', much confusion persisted over what behaviour or whose presence might trigger dispersal.
- Few groups were formally dispersed. In one case study area, during one six-month order, 105 dispersal warnings were given and no arrests were made for breach. In the other case study area, groups were dispersed on 21 occasions, a further 18 groups were formally advised about the powers and eight offences were dealt with.
- Home visits were made to inform the parents of young people dispersed. Some young people were referred to other interventions or diversionary schemes.
- Police mainly used the dispersal powers informally; to facilitate dialogue with young people.
- At least half adult residents believed that the order reduced the number of young people hanging around (56% and 50% respectively in the two case studies); and approximately half said that it had reduced ASB in the area (54% and 46%) and increased perceptions of safety (50% and 47%).
- In one case study area, crime decreased both in comparison with the preceding six months (39%) and the same period the previous year (19%). Criminal damage showed a year-on-year decrease of 52% and a decline of 42% over the previous six months, but in the period after the end of the order it increased by 36%. The number of reported ASB incidents declined by 45% on the previous year.
- In the other case study area, crime decreased during the dispersal order as compared to the preceding six months (by 15.3%), but increased as compared to the same period the previous year (by 9.3%). Criminal damage, however, increased.
- In one neighbouring 'displacement zone', crime rose by 148% on the previous six months and 83% on the previous year, despite police efforts to forestall displacement. Displacement was most apparent for criminal damage.
- In one case study site, over half of the young people surveyed said that the dispersal order had had a negative impact on their feelings towards the local police.
- Many of the young people who said they had been dispersed reported feeling unfairly treated. Half disagreed that the police listened to what they had to say and two fifths said that the experience left them less confident with the police.
- Some 61% of pupils surveyed in one area and 43% in the other said that the dispersal orders were unfairly targeted at young people. Two fifths of young people in both areas thought that the dispersal order had increased conflict between young and old people.
- While wider initiatives accompanied police enforcement strategies, on reflection many felt that more should have been done by way of prevention and diversion, notably with regard to youth provision.

The research highlights the importance of engaging with young people, youth organisations and agencies representing young people both before and after the decision to authorise an area for the purposed of dispersal powers.

The designation of an area as a dispersal zone communicates powerful messages about a place, its values and dominant interests, not least in that the authorisation process requires publicity. The mixed messages that different groups invest in such a controversial and exceptional measure demand careful management.

Interpretation of the powers leaves considerable scope for inconsistent enforcement in ways that can impact negatively on perceptions of fairness and procedural justice. Such dangers are particularly acute where police officers are drafted into an area to bolster visible patrols but who may have less knowledge about the locality.

It is a concern that the presence of groups in a dispersal zone, as much as specific behaviour, may be caught by the dispersal power. In relying on the perceptions of others as a trigger for intervention, dispersal orders potentially criminalise youthful behaviour dependent on the anxieties that young people congregating in groups may generate. The power is potentially less concerned with the agency of the individuals who are the subjects of regulation than the assumptions that are made about what they might do.

In practice, police interpreted and used dispersal powers in a more circumscribed manner than the law might allow. However, this disjuncture between the scope of the law and police practice generated public confusion and the possibility for inconsistent enforcement. For these reasons consideration should be given to bringing the law more in line with current good practice, such that dispersal powers apply only to the *behaviour* of groups rather than merely their *presence*.

Introduction

British neighbourhoods have become more demographically diverse and socially heterogeneous than they were a generation ago. Alongside greater ethnic and cultural diversity, kinship and support structures have also become more varied. Social ties and bonds of mutual obligation have loosened as populations have become more mobile and traditional institutions have declined as forces of social cohesion. Cultural difference has also fostered intergenerational tensions, which frequently get expressed in anxiety about the behaviour of young people. Living together with strangers in relations of mutual respect and tolerance has become one of the central challenges of the modern era. History, however, reminds us that the concerns of a given generation are often projected onto its youth, frequently associated with claims about declining social mores and rising incivility (Pearson, 1982).

Anti-social behaviour (ASB) has become a major political concern and policy preoccupation in recent years. With its genesis in the management of public housing, a range of policies and interventions formulated under the rubric of 'tackling anti-social behaviour' now inform diverse aspects of social life from schooling through to urban planning. In large part, ASB strategies have become focused on the question of governing youth. ASB has come to categorise and demarcate a distinct policy field that blurs and transcends traditional distinctions between crime and disorder, as well as the appropriate use of civil/criminal and formal/informal responses. It constitutes a policy domain in which diverse organisational interests, working assumptions, priorities and multidisciplinary approaches coalesce, often in awkward combinations. At the same time, it introduces the important dimension of 'public perceptions' into issues of local safety, as a result of which fear of crime, public anxieties and community well-being have become prominent concerns in their own right.

As a term, ASB is used to cover a wide range of activities, misdemeanours, incivilities and crimes (sometimes quite serious crimes). It is recognised that people's understanding of what constitutes ASB is 'determined by a series of factors including context, location, community tolerance and quality of life expectations ... what may be considered anti-social behaviour to one person can be seen as acceptable behaviour to another' (Home Office, 2004, p 3). In the Crime and Disorder Act 1998, ASB is defined as behaviour that 'causes or is likely to cause harassment, alarm or distress' to others. This broad definition is both subjective and context specific as it rests on the perceptions of others. This generates difficulties of measurement and meaning, notably between agencies and across localities. ASB, by its nature, does not lie within the remit of any single agency and cuts across traditional legal, organisational and social categories. Many incidences are never reported. Problematically, therefore, new initiatives may encourage greater reporting, and thus appear to inflate the measurement of the problem regardless of any impact on the problem itself.

Nevertheless, crime and ASB have a considerable impact on the lives of many people in Britain with adverse implications for community life and the degradation of public spaces. It can foster a sense of despair and mistrust, which fractures informal relations, encourages those who are able to leave certain areas to move out and erodes the willingness of residents to intervene in support of communal values. Significantly, crime and ASB affect the poorest communities most severely. Where people live is central to experiences and perceptions of ASB. Housing tenure-type also has implications for the types of interventions available to authorities. If, as evidence suggests, concentrated disadvantage is by far the major predictor of urban disorder (Sampson and Raudenbush, 2004), ASB may be as much a symptom of wider neighbourhood inequality, degraded public spaces, failing schools and poor local institutional infrastructures, as it is a stand-alone problem susceptible to a law enforcement-centred response.

The British Crime Survey shows that despite reductions in aggregate crime levels since the mid-1990s, people's anxieties about ASB, low-level incivilities and youth nuisance have continued to increase (see Figure 1). The percentage of the population that perceive young people hanging around in public as a problem increased from 20% to 33% between 1992 and 2006/07. Research reveals that in local neighbourhoods, people are mainly concerned with three issues: general misbehaviour by children and young people; visible drug and alcohol misuse; and neighbour disputes and 'problem families' (Millie et al, 2005). However, there is no simple correspondence between perceptions of risk and actual levels of victimisation. Much of what surveys measure as 'fear of crime' is linked to wider personal feelings of well-being, self-assurance and a sense of control (Farrall et al, 2000).

In 2002, the government launched its Anti-Social Behaviour Strategy and subsequently enacted the 2003 Anti-Social Behaviour Act, introducing a swathe of new powers. In 2006, the government outlined its intention to 'go broader, deeper and further' than before with the establishment of the Respect programme and Taskforce (Home Office, 2006a). Arising from this, it has signalled the next stage policy initiative in its consultation document *Strengthening Powers to Tackle Anti-Social Behaviour* (Home Office, 2006b). Over recent years, a whole new local infrastructure of Crime and Disorder Reduction Partnerships (CDRPs), ASB teams and dedicated coordinators has been established. Alongside this has been the introduction and extension of diverse new technologies of control, including fixed penalty notices for disorder (extended to those aged between 10 and 16), acceptable behaviour contracts, anti-social behaviour orders (ASBOs), anti-social behaviour

Figure 1: British Crime Survey (BCS) trends in crime and perception of ASB

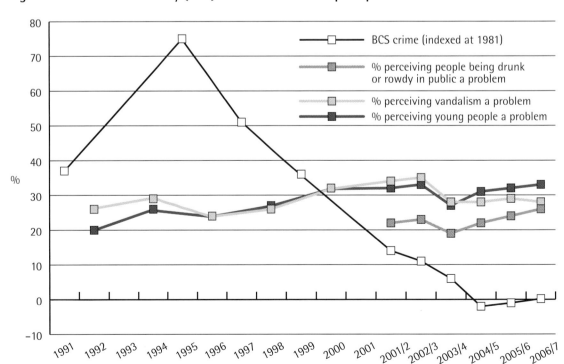

injunctions (ASBIs), child curfew orders, parenting contracts and parenting orders, 'crack house' closure orders, among others. The feverish pace of change has seen the frenetic development and selection of novel institutional tools and their supplement or replacement with newer ones. This proliferation of new powers has left less room for reflection on, and evaluation of, the effectiveness and implications of the powers implemented, as attention rapidly shifts to newer developments. Consequently, little systematic evidence is available regarding the impact and effectiveness of many ASB-related interventions on different groups in the population, as recent reviews have noted (Isal, 2006; YJB, 2006). The National Audit Office (NAO, 2006), for example, described a significant 'knowledge gap' with regard to ASB and the implementation of powers to regulate it. The House of Commons Committee of Public Accounts' report into tackling ASB concluded:

> The lack of published data on the effectiveness of different measures to combat anti-social behaviour in different situations or with different groups of people has led to variation in the extent to which local areas use the interventions available to them. Decisions are based on local preferences and the familiarity of those in authority with the different types of measures, rather than an objective assessment of what works with different types of perpetrators. (2007, p 5)

2

Dispersal order powers and research overview

The idea of dispersal orders was first articulated in the White Paper *Respect and Responsibility*, which sought to outline 'the need for a cultural shift from a society where too many people are living with the consequences of anti-social behaviour, to a society where we respect each other, our property and our shared public spaces' (Home Office, 2003, p 6). To realise this vision, it declared that:

> The police, in consultation with local authorities, will therefore be given the ability to designate areas with significant levels of anti-social behaviour. Within these specified areas the police will be able to disperse groups of people and will have access to automatic, fast-track child curfew powers. (Home Office, 2003, p 53, para 4.13)

The genesis of dispersal orders owes much to a combination of at least four factors. First, there was a distinct frustration on the part of government ministers over the perceived failure of local authorities and the police to use the curfew powers given to them under the 1998 Crime and Disorder Act, and extended under the 2001 Criminal Justice and Police Act. The original power in the 1998 Act allowed for local authorities to apply for local curfew orders for children under 10 in specified areas (ss. 14-15). Subsequently, not one local authority across England and Wales sought to use this power. According to Jack Straw, the then Home Secretary, this was due to an inherent 'conservatism' among local authorities (quoted in House of Commons, 2001, p 40). The 2001 Criminal Justice and Police Act extended the power to apply for a curfew order to local chief police officers (s. 49) and increased the age range to include under-16-year-olds (s. 48). Second, evidence from the British Crime Survey seemed to show an increase in public perceptions of young people hanging about in the street as a big problem in their area (in the decade between 1992 and 2002 the figure increased by 65%, see Figure 1). Third, there was a growing perception that the police were unable to respond adequately to low-level but persistent group-related anti-social activity and intimidatory behaviour. Finally, there was a growing acknowledgement that incivilities significantly affect perceptions of crime, insecurity and fear, and that doing something to combat these 'signal disorders' may produce real benefits for local community well-being and perceptions of personal safety (Innes, 2004).

David Blunkett, Home Secretary at the time of the passage of the 2003 Anti-Social Behaviour Act, explained the genesis of the legislation from a personal perspective:

> 'I was in a public meeting and people were screaming at the police that they weren't doing anything about quite gross behaviour that was really destabilising the community. That was causing those who could to get out and those who remained just to despair as to whether they could live in what they considered to be a basic civilised way. And I said to the police: 'well, what powers would you want?' They said: 'well, we don't want to go back pre-1984 before the Police and Criminal Evidence Act, but the baby was thrown out with the bathwater when the

old unacceptable "sus laws" were abolished and we don't believe we have the power or authority to be able to disperse gangs, to be able to require youngsters to go home when it's clear that they're causing mayhem or there's a danger to others'. And I said: 'well, I'll go back and examine why'. And it was clear that even if they did have powers, they didn't believe that those powers existed or they could use them. So, as part of the Anti-Social Behaviour Act we invented the dispersal and curfew powers.' (Personal interview, January 2007)

Consequently, Part 4 of the 2003 Anti-Social Behaviour Act (ss. 30-36) gives the police in England and Wales new powers to disperse groups of two or more people from areas where there is believed to be persistent ASB and a problem with groups causing intimidation. Within a designated zone a police constable or community support officer (CSO) may disperse groups where their presence or behaviour has resulted, or is likely to result, in a member of the public being harassed, intimidated, alarmed or distressed. The legal authorisation process requires an officer of at least the rank of superintendent:

- to obtain the agreement of the local authority to the proposed authorisation;
- to detail the grounds for authorisation;
- to specify the area covered by the dispersal order and the duration of the authorisation (up to six months);
- to publicise the decision either via a local newspaper or by notices in the area.

The designated area must be clearly defined. At the end of the initial period, designation may be renewed. If it turns out that an order is no longer necessary or proportionate, the police can withdraw the authorisation at any stage pursuant to section 31(6) of the Act, again with the agreement of the local authority.

In an authorised area, a police CSO may give one or more of the following directions:

- tell people in the group to disperse (either immediately, or at a stated time and in a stated way);
- tell people who do not live in the area to leave the area (either immediately, or at a stated time and in a stated way);
- tell people who do not live in the area not to return to the area for a period up to 24 hours.

A person does not commit an offence because an officer has chosen to use the power to disperse, but if individuals refuse to follow the officer's directions, they will be committing an offence, punishable by up to three months' imprisonment and/or a fine of up to £5,000. The role of the authorisation process is to ensure wide consultation and that the designation of the powers is evidenced and proportionate. In recognising the importance of the authorisation process, the court in the case of *Sierny v The Director of Public Prosecutions*[1] held that failure to provide any explanation of the grounds on which an authorisation is based would render the authorisation invalid. However, the courts have also held that an authorisation granted on specific grounds does not restrain the subsequent powers being used in relation to other forms of ASB. In the case of *Singh*,[2] it was held that so long as their use is proportionate, there does not need to be a direct relationship between the grounds for the initial authorisation.

The Act provides additional powers for dealing with those aged under 16 years old (s. 30(6)). Where a police constable believes such a person to be in the authorised area between the hours of 9pm and 6am and without a parent or responsible adult, he or

---

[1] Sierny v The Director of Public Prosecutions [2006] EWHC 716.
[2] Singh v Chief Constable of West Midlands Police [2006] EWCA Civ 1118.

she may remove the child to their home address.[3] The local authority must be informed when this power is used. This element of the legislation, variously known as the 'curfew' or 'escort power', was the subject of an early legal judgement in July 2005, in which the High Court ruled that the power did not allow the use of reasonable force.[4] Consequently, police forces around the country suspended the use of the power. However, in May 2006 the Court of Appeal overturned the earlier judgement but laid down two conditions for the exercise of reasonable force under the original power.[5] Young people can only be removed to their home from a dispersal order zone if they are either (i) at risk or vulnerable from ASB and crime or (ii) causing (or at risk of causing) ASB.

In the light of this, new guidance was published (Home Office, 2006c) and the then Home Office Minister, Tony McNulty, challenged police and practitioners 'to take a more robust and unremitting approach to tackling anti-social behaviour by making maximum use of the dispersal powers available to them' (Home Office Press Release 30 June 2006).[6] The power to escort home is unavailable in Scotland, partly because of concerns raised about its coercive nature and potential conflict with wider child welfare policies. As Table 1 shows, there are several significant differences between the powers available in England and Wales as compared to Scotland.

Table 1: England and Wales, and Scotland compared

	England and Wales	Scotland
Legislative basis	2003 Anti-Social Behaviour Act	2004 Anti-Social Behaviour etc (Scotland) Act
Commencement date	20 January 2004	October 2004
Duration of designation	Up to six months (renewable)	Up to three months (renewable)
Who can use the powers?	Powers extend to police CSOs	No equivalent to CSOs in Scotland, only police constable
Extent of powers	Escort power to return home a young person under 16 who is out on the streets between 9pm and 6am, not under adult control	No equivalent power
Penalties available for breach	A fine of up to £5,000 and/or imprisonment of up to three months	A fine of up to £2,500 and/or imprisonment of up to three months
Monitoring	Since April 2006 by way of quarterly returns from the police	Six-monthly reports from Association of Chief Police Officers in Scotland (ACPOS)
Evaluation requirement	No equivalent requirement to evaluate implementation or effectiveness	Requirement on Scottish ministers to conduct a study into the operation of dispersal powers and lay it before Parliament within three years of the powers' commencement (Part 3, s. 24)

---

[3] Unless the police officer has reasonable grounds for believing that the child if removed to that place would be likely to suffer significant harm.

[4] R (On the Application of W) v Commissioner of Police of the Metropolis and Richmond Borough Council [2005] EWCA Civ 1568: Queens Bench Division.

[5] R (W) v Commissioner of Police of the Metropolis and others [2006] EWCA Civ 458: Court of Appeal.

[6] See http://press.homeoffice.gov.uk/press-releases/anti-social-behaviour

In Scotland, unlike England and Wales, there was considerable public debate and criticism prior to and during the introduction of the powers into legislation. Over 80% of responses to the consultation *Putting Our Communities First: A Strategy for tackling Anti-Social Behaviour* opposed the introduction of dispersal orders, believing that the police already had sufficient powers (Flint et al, 2003, p 109). This included the Association of Chief Police Officers of Scotland (ACPOS) and the Scottish Police Federation (SPF). ACPOS, among others, argued that there was a danger that all gatherings of young people would become labelled as problematic. The SPF feared that new powers would raise public expectations in a context of a lack of police resources. Other concerns included singling out and unfairly targeting young people in potentially stigmatising ways and that the powers may impact adversely on relations between young people and the police. Consequently, the debate both within the Scottish Parliament and in the wider media was more apparent than in England and Wales.

More recently, a variant of the dispersal order power has been introduced to disperse people to avoid a risk of future drink-related disorder, under the 2006 Violent Crime Reduction Act (s. 27). In November 2006, the Home Office (2006b) published a consultation paper seeking views on proposals for further powers to tackle ASB. One of the proposals is to introduce a new frontline power that will allow police to disperse individuals without the need for prior designation of a given area. This proposed on-the-spot power would significantly extend current dispersal orders, allowing officers to require an individual to keep away from a particular area for a certain time (possibly longer than 24 hours). The consultation paper argued that: 'Police officers have asked for powers to take swift, preventative action against anti-social behaviour, where the offender's behaviour was not of the degree to merit an ASBO.... Such powers ... would be at the discretion of a police officer, and could potentially have a strong deterrent effect on others' (Home Office, 2006b, p 11). It is anticipated that new legislation to take forward these proposals will be forthcoming.

Research overview

The findings reported here were conducted over a 12-month fieldwork period from 1 April 2006 to 31 March 2007. The research aimed to:

- understand the extent to which dispersal orders help address the problems that give rise to their implementation;
- provide an understanding of the processes involved in implementing dispersal orders and identify good practice;
- assess the impact of the use of dispersal orders and their effectiveness in reducing crime and ASB;
- explore the role and use of dispersal orders in regulating ASB in the context of, and in relation to, other ASB-related preventative and law enforcement interventions.

It was intended that the findings should inform policy debate and practice developments.

The findings draw on data from three principal sources:

(1) *a national overview:* based on interviews with police and local authority practitioners from across the UK, as well as national policy makers;
(2) *two city-based studies in Sheffield and Leeds:* these considered the development of strategies over time, the distribution of orders across a city and the longer-term impact of specific orders;
(3) *two case studies, one in Yorkshire and one in Outer London:* in each site six-month dispersal orders were studied from authorisation through to completion.

Research methods

The research data were collected by way of:

National overview

- eight interviews with prominent national politicians, policy makers, civil liberties campaigners and civil servants;
- 17 interviews with police, ASB coordinators and council employees involved in local implementation across 13 police force areas.

In the two city sites:

- nine interviews with management and frontline police officers;
- five interviews with local authority staff and other key stakeholders;
- one focus group interview with five young people.

In the case studies:

- surveys of 830 residents living in or adjacent to the two dispersal zones; 273 from the Yorkshire site and 557 from the London site;
- surveys of 573 pupils from two schools located close to the boundaries of the case study areas; 199 in Yorkshire and 374 in London;
- 12 focus group interviews with a total of 104 young people;
- 16 interviews with residents and local businesses;
- 23 interviews with management and frontline police officers;
- 18 interviews with other key professional stakeholders – council officials, ASB coordinators, youth workers and housing staff;
- six hours of observations of community and residents' groups meetings;
- 30 hours of police observations over 12 separate shifts to observe implementation. These observations were concentrated in the early weeks of each dispersal order when activity was at its most intense (including observation in the city sites).

To ensure the agreed confidentiality of all research participants and to minimise any adverse impact of the research on particular localities, where appropriate we have removed references to specific places or people and anonymised the case study sites, which are referred to by way of pseudonyms.

3

National overview

This chapter draws on national data from both the Home Office and the Scottish Executive to provide an overview of the use of dispersal orders in Britain since their introduction in 2004. Recent police data from across London are presented. These quantitative data are supplemented by interviews with police and local authority practitioners with experience of implementing dispersal orders, as well as national policy makers. The discussion focuses on the lessons learnt through implementation, regarding the benefits, challenges and pitfalls of using dispersal orders, together with implications for best practice.

England and Wales

National data on the use of dispersal orders in England and Wales were initially collected by way of Home Office surveys of all Crime and Disorder Reduction Partnerships (CDRPs). Three survey rounds were conducted. As they cover overlapping timescales and response rates were variable and patchy, the data cannot easily be combined. The surveys revealed that 234 dispersal orders were authorised in the initial period between 20 January and 31 August 2004. The second survey showed that by the end of June 2005 over 800 designated areas had been authorised. Of these, three forces accounted for a quarter of all areas designated, whereas four forces had designated none and five had designated only one. Over a quarter (27%) of orders had been renewed or redesignated (Home Office, 2005).

The most recent national survey elicited responses from 214 of 373 CDRPs in England and Wales (a 57.4% response rate). It found that a total of 1,065 areas were designated dispersal zones between 20 January 2004 and 31 March 2006 (see Figure 2). The data show a steep decline in the use of dispersal orders in 2005/06 after some considerable take-up in 2004/5,

Figure 2: Number of dispersal orders in England and Wales (April–March), by year

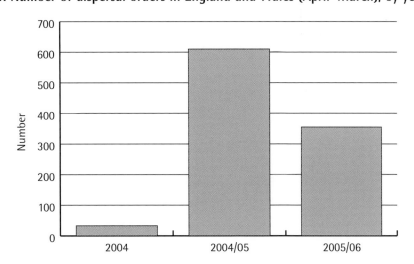

Note: Dispersal orders were introduced 20 January 2004; hence, data for 2004 represent less than three months.
Source: Home Office (2007a)

representing a 42% reduction in use (from 610 to 355). The dispersal order was the only ASB-related intervention to decline in use, comparing starkly with considerable increases over the same period in the take-up of other measures, such as acceptable behaviour contracts, parenting contracts/orders, ASB injunctions, demotion orders and 'crack house' closures (Home Office, 2007a).

The data shown in Figure 2 appear to confirm our research findings that since the inception of dispersal orders, many senior police and local authority officers have become more aware of the limitations of the powers on the basis of operational experiences. The initial flurry of activity has been tempered by an acknowledgement of the challenges that dispersal orders bring and the types of places and problems for which they work least well. The downturn in use also reflects a more general preference among many community safety and ASB practitioners to prioritise preventative approaches over enforcement. A survey of 1,000 practitioners conducted for the Respect Taskforce in June 2007 found that when asked what, if anything, over the last three years has made the most difference to their work tackling ASB, the most common response was 'better partnership working' (Ipsos Mori, 2007). Nearly twice as many practitioners identified this factor compared to those who suggested that the new enforcement tools available (for example, ASBOs, acceptable behaviour contracts (ABCs), warning letters, injunctions and dispersal orders) had made the most difference.

Scotland

Largely as a result of the contentious nature of public debate about the appropriateness of the new orders, senior police officers in Scotland were initially reluctant to use the powers. Within the first 18 months following their introduction in October 2004, only four dispersal orders were implemented. These first orders generated a high level of publicity and some negative press coverage. By February 2007, some 14 dispersal zones had been designated in Scotland covering 11 locations (see Figure 3). In two areas the same location was the subject of subsequent orders; a total of three authorisations in relation to Hunter Square in Edinburgh and two for Beach Boulevard, Aberdeen (see Box 8 on p 18). Thus, just over one fifth of all Scottish orders to date have been renewals.

So far, two of the eight Scottish Constabularies (Fife and Tayside) have not used dispersal orders. Nevertheless, as Figure 3 shows, their use is now increasing, by contrast with England and Wales. A civil servant in the Scottish Executive described the lagged nature of developments in Scotland: 'It's a more softly, softly approach here, just to see how it

Figure 3: Number of dispersal orders in Scotland, by year

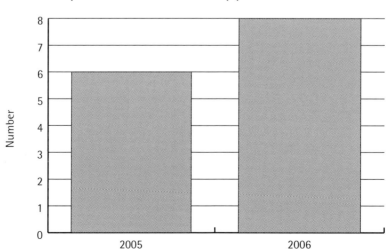

goes'. Generally, Scotland has adopted a more cautious stance towards a variety of ASB-related orders (including parenting orders and ASBOs), preferring a voluntary approach, at least in the first instance, rather than direct legal intervention. Nonetheless, it is with some irony that the post-devolution period has seen considerable legal and institutional convergence between Scotland and England and Wales of both youth justice generally and the regulation of ASB specifically (McAra, 2005).

Additional reasons given for the different take-up of dispersal orders north of the border include:

- the different cultural and legal approach in Scotland, which stresses a reluctance to use criminalisation as a means of managing youth problems, as enshrined in the Kilbrandon philosophy and the children's hearing system;[7]
- community safety partnerships developed along a different trajectory, nestled alongside wider social, urban and youth policy agendas rather than a narrow crime and disorder framework as apparent in England and Wales;
- the reluctance of police officers of the rank of superintendent personally to authorise dispersal orders given both the hesitancy from among police chiefs over their effectiveness and superintendents' relative lack of experience in authorising such powers in Scotland.

London

Given its population, it is unsurprising that more dispersal orders have been authorised in the Metropolitan Police area than in any other force in Britain. Across its jurisdiction, 61 dispersal notices were authorised in 2004, including all but six London boroughs. Some 39 (that is, 64%) were designated for reasons of youth disorder. As a result, 3,312 people were dispersed, 116 arrested for breach and 145 under-16-year-olds returned home. Escort powers were used in only 18 of the 39 youth-related dispersal order areas (46%), with three dispersal order areas accounting for 102 (70%) of those escorted home. Police analysis of the use of powers in 2004 shows that:

- approximately 60% of all people dispersed were under 18;
- 85% dispersed were male;
- 20% dispersed were recorded as being Black (as compared with census data across London of 11%);
- of the 116 arrests these were equally split between those 'refusing to leave' and 'returning';
- 94% of those arrested were male;
- 28% of those arrested were recorded as being Black (although numbers are low).

Metropolitan Police data show that within the London area 85 dispersal orders ended between 1 April 2006 and 31 March 2007.[8] The average length of these was almost 22 weeks (Figure 4). Nearly two thirds (62%) of orders were for the maximum duration eligible under the legislation of 26 weeks (that is, six months).

---

[7] Named after the chair of a committee set up to review youth justice in early 1960, the subsequent report (Kilbrandon Committee, 1964) stressed early and minimal intervention avoiding stigmatisation through criminalisation, with an emphasis on the needs of children rather than their (mis)deeds. The system of children's hearing panels, introduced some years after the publication of the report, encapsulates this philosophy.

[8] Data are submitted to the Home Office on completed dispersal orders only.

Figure 4: Duration of dispersal orders in London 2006/07 in weeks (*n*=85)

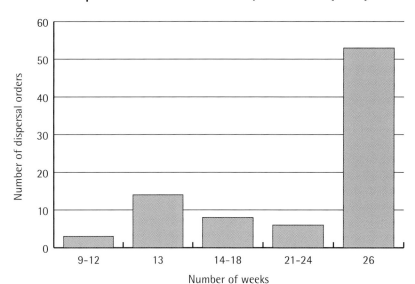

Over a third (34%) of all dispersal orders were authorised within residential areas, but the majority (51%) were located in either shopping areas or city/town centre locations (Figure 5). More than a third (36%) were in areas that had been previously designated a dispersal zone. One area had been designated on six previous occasions and in a further eight areas designation had been renewed either three or four times.

Figure 6 shows that the reason given for nearly three quarters (73%) of all dispersal orders in London was either general ASB caused by groups or general non-specific ASB. A further 15% of orders related to drug or substance misuse and dealing or street drinking.

The data on the number of people dispersed were available for almost half the dispersal orders (42 of 85). Although incomplete, these data show a highly variable pattern of use of the powers. A total of 4,888 people were dispersed from the 42 areas, an average of 116 per dispersal zone. However, only three orders, akin to 5% of the total, accounted for more than half (54%) of all people dispersed (some 2,633 in total). Two of these orders were a renewal in the same residential area, which alone accounted for 1,853 dispersals (38% of the total), with the other covering a large commercial area in the West End. All three of

Figure 5: Type of location

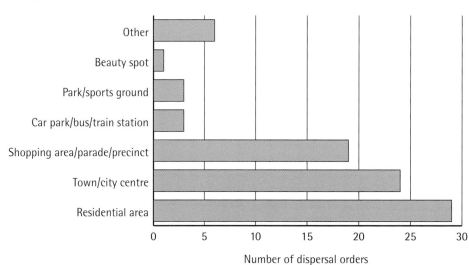

Figure 6: Reasons given for designation

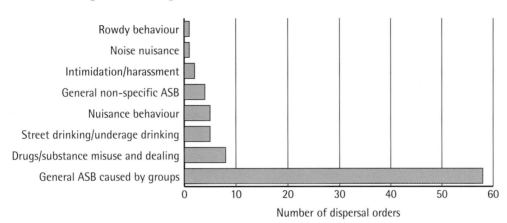

these orders were for six months. The data show that the escort powers were recorded as having been used only in two areas and on four occasions.

Lessons from practice

The development of the order over time

Our interviews suggest that the last three years have been a learning curve for police and local authorities. Unlike Scotland, in England and Wales dispersal powers were greeted with some enthusiasm, albeit mixed with a dose of uncertainty, as a new tool that practitioners were willing to experiment with in order to explore its potential utility in addressing ASB. It has been largely through the experience of implementation that best practice lessons have been learnt and the limitations of dispersal powers have become more apparent. Evidence suggests that dispersal orders are most frequently used to cover the summer and autumn months, largely because the seasonal conditions lend themselves to young people gathering in groups in public spaces.

Nature of the problem – grounds for designation

Our overview of developments, supported by the Home Office surveys, shows that youth disorder is overwhelmingly the most prominent trigger for dispersal orders. Nevertheless, dispersal orders have also been used to address a diversity of types of crime and ASB including racially motivated attacks and racist harassment (see Box 1), attacks on asylum seekers, vandalism (see Box 2), drug dealing (see Box 5), alcohol-related violence (see Box 6), illegal trading, misuse of fireworks (Sheffield case study, see Chapter 4), street robbery (see Box 7), vehicle-related disorder (see Box 8), 'aggressive' street begging and prostitution.

Box 1: Racially motivated crime, Outer London

A dispersal order was introduced for Halloween night in relation to a specific street in 2004 and 2005. The aim of the order was to protect an Asian family from racially motivated attacks. The family had been the subject of racial harassment, damage to their property and fireworks being thrown at their premises on the evening of Halloween. A 24-hour dispersal order was introduced to cover that night alone. The order was used to disperse both known and suspected racist groups from gathering in the street in which the home was situated. The order was enforced by a partnership between Metropolitan Police, British Transport Police and Parks Police, as the premises were situated close to a large park and Underground station. In 2004, 16 stops were made. There were no criminal attacks on the vulnerable premises. In 2005, 12 stops were made and two stop and searches. Again, there were no criminal attacks on the property. The perceived success of the order resulted in it not being renewed in 2006.

Type of location

Designated areas vary significantly in size and can be as large or as small as required. Dispersal orders have been used in zones as tightly confined as a specific street (see Box 1), a church and graveyard (see Box 2) and a designated shopping arcade. By contrast, whole city centres, such as Leeds (see Chapter 4) and the West End of London, as well as an entire community (see Box 3), have been designated a dispersal zone. There have also been joint and cross-border initiatives between neighbouring local authorities and police forces (see Box 4).

Box 2: Vandalism to churches, Dumphries

St. Michael's and St. Andrew's churches in Dumphries were the subject of two separate but related dispersal orders from April to July 2006. Both orders were in response to reports from church leaders and congregations of incidents of vandalism and graffiti, which had apparently worsened over a number of years. Both churches are located near the town centre and were used as a congregation place for local youths. St Michael's Church has a large graveyard, which contains the Burns Mausoleum where the remains of Robert Burns and his family are kept. The Mausoleum was itself the subject of attack. During the order a total of 11 people were dispersed and no arrests were made for breach.

Duration

The data suggest that initially most dispersal orders were authorised for the maximum 6-month period. More recently, in many parts of the country, police and council staff have become more inclined to opt for shorter, more tailored designation periods. It is evident that these shorter designation periods then become subject to a formal review before being renewed, where deemed necessary. Some of the reasons given for this shift towards shorter orders include:

- *resources* – they are more manageable and less resource intensive for the police to provide the required additional patrols;
- *community expectations* – they better allow aims to be clarified and residents' aspirations of success to be more realistically grounded; and
- *partnership buy-in* – they necessitate partner agencies to act quickly and decisively in planning longer-term coordinated strategies.

Box 3: West Lothian

In West Lothian, an entire village became the subject of a dispersal order between December 2005 and February 2006. A relatively affluent village containing several pubs and comprising a population of approximately 3,000, it routinely experienced alcohol-related disorder at weekends, which was believed to be caused by non-resident youths. Complaints were made to the police about groups of up to 50 young people congregating in the village on weekend evenings. One incident led to three young people being charged with attempted murder after a youth suffered a fractured skull. During authorisation the order was only in effect at weekends between 5pm on Friday until midnight on

Sunday. It was primarily aimed as a defensive strategy to deter groups of young people choosing to use the village as a meeting place. During the period 72 formal dispersals were issued and no arrests were made for breach of dispersal directions. The order was seen by the police as a success, as calls for service fell and little displacement to neighbouring villages was evident. Unfortunately, the village was labelled the 'village of the banned' by the press.

The same reasoning has also had similar implications for the scale or size of dispersal order areas, which in many instances have become smaller and more refined. However, there are significant countervailing pressures to increase the size of dispersal zones where the authorisation process involves wide-ranging consultation that either identifies concerns about displacement or related problems in neighbouring areas (see Chapter 4).

Box 4: Joint dispersal order, Inner London

Police in Camden and Westminster launched a joint dispersal order in the summer of 2006 to address drug-related problems, notably street dealing, in areas that were close to the respective borders of both boroughs. The joint order facilitated greater coordination of policing and related activities. In part, it arose out of a frustration with earlier initiatives that had largely served to displace the problem across the border into the neighbouring borough.

Authorisation

The exceptional nature of the powers triggered by a dispersal order necessitates a process of authorisation. This process (Figure 7) should ensure that the order is evidenced and proportionate to the nature and extent of the ASB problem. Where conducted rigorously the process of authorisation provides dispersal powers a degree of legitimacy and public accountability. Our research suggests that the rigours that attach to the process are variously interpreted. In some instances, considerable emphasis has been given to the information base on which an application is founded. In others, however, the process was accorded less significance and on occasions was viewed less robustly, as 'boxes to be ticked', rather than an essential bedrock on which the efficacy and veracity of designation is founded.

Evidence

According to legislation, the evidence required must show 'persistent' ASB and a problem with groups causing intimidation in the area to be designated. Evidence gathering is often restricted to police data on ASB-related calls for service and ASB incidents. Inevitably, police data suffer problems of under-reporting and recording, particularly evident for ASB. The collation of information may initiate specific data-mapping exercises and incorporate additional ASB data held by partner agencies, such as the local authority or social housing associations, and/or the use of surveys of local residents and businesses.

These additional forms of data should not be used to circumvent the absence of evidence contained in police data in order to construct a case for authorisation, but rather to provide further confirmation and fuller evidence of a prima facie case already evidenced in police data. This research uncovered examples where alternative sources of data were used to 'prop up' an otherwise weak evidence base revealed through police-recorded data. Given the exceptional status of the powers, it is important that 'evidence' should be restricted to incidents that highlight the *persistence* of ASB within the area and the existence of a

Figure 7: Authorisation process

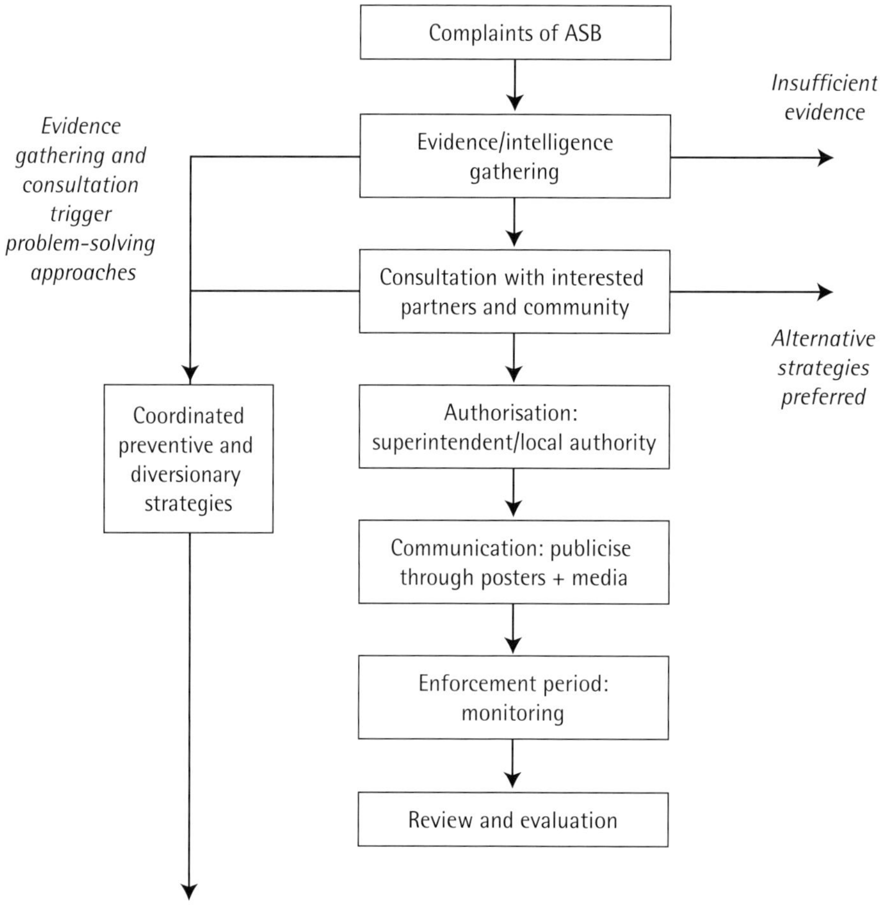

```
                              ┌──────────────────────┐
                              │  Complaints of ASB   │
                              └──────────┬───────────┘
                                         │
                                         ▼                          Insufficient
      Evidence              ┌──────────────────────┐                evidence
   gathering and      ┌─────│  Evidence/intelligence│───────────────────────►
   consultation       │     │      gathering        │
     trigger          │     └──────────┬───────────┘
 problem-solving       │                │
   approaches          │                ▼
                       │     ┌──────────────────────┐
                       └─────│ Consultation with     │───────────────────────►
                             │ interested partners   │
                             │    and community      │              Alternative
                             └──────────┬───────────┘                strategies
                                         │                            preferred
         ┌──────────────────┐            ▼
         │  Coordinated     │  ┌──────────────────────┐
         │  preventive and  │  │ Authorisation:       │
         │  diversionary    │  │ superintendent/local │
         │  strategies      │  │ authority            │
         └────────┬─────────┘  └──────────┬───────────┘
                  │                        │
                  │                        ▼
                  │             ┌──────────────────────┐
                  │             │ Communication:        │
                  │             │ publicise through     │
                  │             │ posters + media       │
                  │             └──────────┬───────────┘
                  │                        │
                  │                        ▼
                  │             ┌──────────────────────┐
                  │             │ Enforcement period:   │
                  │             │ monitoring            │
                  │             └──────────┬───────────┘
                  │                        │
                  │                        ▼
                  │             ┌──────────────────────┐
                  ▼             │ Review and evaluation │
                                └──────────────────────┘
```

problem with groups *causing* intimidation, rather than documentation on the perceptions of some local residents and businesses or their preferences for certain enforcement-based policing strategies.

Box 5: Drug dealing, Bristol

In December 2004 a six-month dispersal order was authorised to cover a whole area of the city to help tackle the street-level drug trade. The order was renewed three times, establishing a continuous 18-month order. Responsibility for enforcing the order rested mostly with community officers supported by the Drugs and Robbery team. The order was enforced flexibly to address other forms of ASB (for example, problem street drinking). Displacement of drug dealing was restricted by the extensive coverage of the designated area, and because a dispersal order was running concurrently in a neighbouring area. In addition, a range of other ASB tools was used, including several successful applications for the closure of 'crack houses' and ASBOs imposed on individuals identified as persistent offenders.

In some instances, applications have not been taken forward by the commanding police superintendent who must assess the weight of the evidence in light of other operational resource demands. In this context, the extent of the problem may be deemed insufficient to justify authorisation. In one South Yorkshire town, for instance, despite initially preparing an application for a dispersal order, the police subsequently decided not to pursue it on the basis of resource implications and uncertainties over outcomes. Instead, more traditional policing strategies were preferred:

'We started the process by getting impact statements from residents to get a dispersal order. We think we probably would have got one but we just weren't convinced of the effect. We'd only got a few offenders, so we thought just to target these few offenders would be as good as actually having a dispersal order. So for the past month with local police officers and PCSOs we've basically flooded the area; and it is quite a small area. If ultimately the problem continues, we might have to look at the dispersal order again. But, we're still not convinced it's the ideal place to have it.' (Middle-ranking officer, South Yorkshire Police)

Box 6: Alcohol-related violence, North East

In April 2005 a five-week dispersal order was introduced within Middlesbrough town centre to address alcohol-related violence and ASB. The order sought to provide a safer trading environment for the town's pub and club trade. The timing of the dispersal order intentionally coincided with the May Bank holiday weekends, when traditionally the town centre has attracted large numbers of drinkers, resulting in increased disorder. Police used the dispersal order as a formal and proactive means of excluding drinkers from the town centre for 24 hours. It was introduced alongside a range of other enforcement and preventive measures. These included operations targeted at off-licensed premises found to be selling alcohol to people under age and those in an inebriated state.

In some places, applications have failed to gain local approval because the police and/or partners have decided to implement alternative strategies that are considered to be less contentious and longer-term in focus:

'[The] police were considering doing another dispersal order, however, they had done quite a bit of research into what the problems actually were and felt they didn't need to do a dispersal order. They went in and they did an awful lot of other intervention work. And they have looked at that as being good practice for them.' (Local authority officer, Cumbria)

In other instances, police applications have been turned down or deferred by senior local authority officers, who are required to co-sign authorisation. Although there is often pressure to use dispersal orders from elected councillors, the research encountered a growing reticence over their use among council officers with experience of overseeing implementation elsewhere.

Box 7: Robbery and street crime, Inner London

A 12-week dispersal order between July and September 2004 aimed to reduce robbery and street crime around the Camden Lock area, where markets attract many young people and tourists. Traditionally the area has a high incidence of street crime and drug dealing. In advance of the dispersal order a 'positive charge' policy was agreed between the police and Crown Prosecution Service for those found breaching dispersal directives. During the initiative, 134 dispersal notices were issued and 12 people arrested in accordance with the charging policy. Most of those individuals dispersed resided outside the borough of Camden. Compared to the same period the previous year, reported robbery and snatch theft reduced by 35% and drug-related calls to the police declined by 27%. An application by the police to extend the order initially failed, but a new six-month order was authorised for the area in mid-2006.

Early and extensive consultation between the police, local authorities and other key organisations is crucial in attaining consensus over whether introducing a dispersal order is justified. Increasingly, providing an adequate foundation for these grounds requires a rigorous examination of alternative strategies and the development of long-term problem-

Box 8: Aberdeen

Scotland's first dispersal order, which began in March 2005, was implemented along the Beach Boulevard area, a stretch of road adjacent to the seafront. The Boulevard was traditionally used as a gathering place for young motorists, known locally as 'Bouley Bashers', who congregated in their modified cars, motorbikes and scooters. In 2004, 266 calls of complaint were made by local residents regarding noise from music, cars and people and road traffic offences, as well as other associated disorder. During the initial three-month period 62 formal dispersals were issued and two arrests for breach were made. This resulted in two individuals being charged, convicted and given 12-month suspended sentences. Grampian Police recorded a 53% drop in reported incidents of ASB during the designated period. The initial order was renewed for a further three months.

solving partnerships and preventive approaches. This allows, for instance, the application for a dispersal order to progress alongside applications to fund complementary measures.

Equally, it is important that police and local authorities fully engage with young people, youth organisations, voluntary agencies representing young people and, notably, the new local multi-agency Children's Trusts[9] both before and after authorisation. Such engagement can be explanatory in outlook, but also inclusive and consultative. Many police authorities now commission surveys of their local communities, with a view to gaining information about perceptions of local problems and opinions on suggested solutions. As the following officer explained, such preliminary work can provide a dispersal order with legitimacy and the police with a clear mandate:

'The police authority thought there was a big issue, so every household got the same survey through the letterbox.... From that, 98% of people wanted a dispersal order in respect to the rowdy young people. So we had a bit of a mandate, a bit of a steer, well quite a large steer from the community. We then held a focus group with 40 invited people and debriefed them and it was quite clear what they wanted was a dispersal order.' (Middle-ranking officer, South Yorkshire Police)

Communication challenges

Many practitioners lauded the value of effective communication to clarify the aims and limitations of the dispersal order and to dispel any misunderstandings about the proposed powers, intentions and implementation strategies. While the law demands that the grounds for the order and its boundaries be publicised either via a local newspaper or by notices displayed in the area, communication is best regarded as an essential aspect of the process, rather than a minimum legislative requirement. Most practitioners felt that both forms of publicity constituted the very minimum and that more extensive forms of communication were necessary to limit public confusion, manage expectations and avoid conflict. In areas with significant non-English-speaking residents, consideration needs to be given how best to publicise and communicate the powers and implications of the dispersal order.

---

[9] Children's Trusts bring together all services for children and young people in an area, underpinned by the 2004 Children Act duty to cooperate (s. 10), to focus on improving the well-being of children in line with the philosophy informing *Every Child Matters* (DfES, 2003). A key element of Children's Trusts is a requirement of the local authority and its partners to develop a strategic plan – referred to as the Children and Young People's Plan (s. 17 of the Act). The five *Every Child Matters* outcomes are: to be healthy; stay safe; enjoy and achieve; make a positive contribution; and achieve economic well-being.

As part of communication strategies in some dispersal areas, the police handed out leaflets in the designated zones explaining the powers. These were used as a prompt to a wider discussion about appropriate behaviour, while offering an informal warning to individuals and groups whose future behaviour might be considered anti-social or who might be in danger of breaching the order. Some police forces issued notices to individuals when they were being formally dispersed. These notices were largely designed as evidential support in any subsequent contested court cases concerning breach of dispersal directions.

Managing the media representation of a dispersal order was often an unexpectedly time-consuming element. One police officer outlined the 'communication battle' that many said they had experienced with the media:

> 'The press have probably been the worst culprit in that they will report something, a particular spate of crime and habitually add on "despite the fact there's a dispersal order enforced".... And it can be anything. It can be a bunch of cars broken into or something like that, tagged on, "despite the fact there's a dispersal order enforced". I've tried to hammer it home to people all the way through, a dispersal order is not a tool to tackle vehicle crime.' (Middle-ranking officer, North Yorkshire Police)

Clear communication to police officers regarding implementation policies was central to consistent enforcement strategies:

> 'Another issue was raising the awareness of the powers amongst officers because it's a brand new power, nobody knows what their actual powers are so we had to develop an *aide mémoire* for officers, just to explain the powers in very simplistic terms what they could do, what they couldn't do.' (Middle-ranking officer, Staffordshire Police)

Uncertainties on the part of officers could serve to fuel local misunderstandings and confusions.

Impact on police resources

The main costs of implementation are those attributed to police staffing. Most police forces had not quantified the precise amount of additional police staff time dedicated to the policing of a dispersal order. Several, however, reported the impact on resources as being more than they had anticipated in advance:

> 'It was very labour intensive. I dread to think what it cost in overtime because we needed to put out somewhere in the region of six officers each evening. It's no good having the legislation if you then don't have the staff to be able to actually enforce it.' (Middle-ranking officer, Cumbria Police)

Most police used neighbourhood policing teams to implement dispersal orders, making it especially difficult to assess the extent to which the policing cover was genuinely additional. Some forces drew additional resources from an overtime budget; others restructured shift patterns in order to free-up staff time to be able to increase the level of patrol in the dispersal zone. In one location, the police reported that an extra 2,000 staff hours had been dedicated to policing a three-month dispersal period. This level of resource deployment is likely to be difficult to sustain and may also have knock-on implications for neighbouring communities. Some police officers, reflecting on their experience of dispersal orders, said that in the future they might think twice before repeating the exercise because of the significant impact on police resources:

'We can only sustain this for a three-month period. We're going to have to find different ways of dealing with problems in this area other than throwing police resources at it, which is always a quick fix.' (Middle-ranking officer, West Yorkshire Police)

In other areas, experience of the complexities and resource implications that attend to implementing a dispersal order, combined with its stigmatising potential, led police not to seek to renew an order even where the ASB problems had not been resolved:

'Now the problem with the power was in order to use it properly, you're required to take details of the individuals that you're dispersing, know whether they live in or outside the zone, tell them whether you want them to stay out for 24 hours or whether to just disperse … that was useful in its own right but it made the measurement of the success of the use of that dispersal order very, very difficult, which is why we decided not to renew, to see whether we could just use [normal] police powers. If that was having the same effect, did we need to have a dispersal order that effectively labels a community with this anti-social behaviour brush?' (Middle-ranking officer, Avon and Somerset Police)

Implementation strategies

Most frontline police officers were pleased to have the additional flexibility that the dispersal powers conferred on them, particularly at a time when many felt, more generally, that their scope for discretion was being curtailed in other areas of police-work:

'I think the fact that we can use discretion and be sensible with it is great.' (Middle-ranking officer, Metropolitan Police)

It provides them with formal authority to do what many considered to be a key aspect of traditional policing; namely engaging with groups of young people, negotiating order and asking them to move on if their behaviour is causing offence to others. Where negotiation fails, it endows them an ultimate course of action.

Almost all dispersal orders examined for this research pursued an enforcement strategy that aimed to have an immediate, noticeable impact through intensive visible patrols. This 'big bang' approach was designed to coincide with publicity and send a clear message to potential offenders and the community. The following comment reflects the approach of many:

'We got some money, we put lots of resources [in place] and over the first three weeks we went out and used it an awful lot in order to make a quick impact and for people to see us using it.' (Middle-ranking officer, Avon and Somerset Police)

However, this approach also raised questions over the extent to which police were able to sustain that level of commitment. Some police advocated an enforcement strategy that emphasised arrest in all instances where dispersal directions were breached. This 'aggressive' enforcement strategy was more common where ASB-related problems were believed to derive from non-local residents. The intention was to send out an unequivocal deterrent message; encouraging potential troublemakers to 'keep out' or face formal police action. In most other areas police preferred a more cautious approach, opting to use dispersal and arrest powers as a tool of last resort. A police manager explained the typical thinking behind such an approach:

'The policy is where you see a group of youths on the street, you engage with them first of all; talk to them, find out what they're doing. Explain to them what their presence means for the rest of the community, how people may feel intimidated by them. And try to engage and explain to the young people the problem they are causing. The next part is to direct them towards the youth provision in the area. The third strand is, if all of that fails and they're causing anti-social behaviour, then you can direct them out of the area by using your powers.' (Middle-ranking officer, West Yorkshire Police)

In some areas, notably town and city centres, dispersal powers enabled police officers to target specific known offenders without interfering with other people's use of public spaces:

'We didn't want officers to think this was a carte blanche power just to split up people who were doing nothing. We wanted them to be focused on individuals. We know who's causing the problems. So those individuals were highlighted as of interest to us during the operation. It's not a carte blanche curfew. We're not targeting people going about legitimate business. We're looking at specific targets that are causing specific problems, in specific areas.' (Middle-ranking officer, Staffordshire Police)

In city centre operations, it was often deemed neither necessary nor practical to publicise the existence of the dispersal powers to all those who frequented the area.

Police were aware that once word spread of a dispersal order's existence, the mere presence of officers was sufficient to prompt groups to disperse, regardless of what they might have been doing. In this way, self-imposed informal dispersal frequently occurred. Where formal police action ensued, the details of individuals involved were to be recorded by the intervening police officer or CSO. As such, dispersal powers, while triggered by past incidents of ASB, also served as a means of prospectively collecting information about individuals present within designated zones. On occasions, this element of intelligence gathering was an explicit part of the policing strategy:

'We know there's a huge problem there, residents tell us. [But] we don't necessarily know all of the people that are going there to cause a problem. So [the dispersal order] can then sometimes be put in as a short-term information-gathering exercise to find out who all of those individuals are.' (Middle-ranking officer, Avon and Somerset Police)

A recurring police challenge was to identify individuals who might have breached dispersal directives. This problem is made more difficult by shift changes and where outside teams of officers are brought into an area to enforce an order. Again, local beat managers and officers with considerable local knowledge were in the best position to address these challenges. Some police forces used mobile and hand-held CCTV to assist the identification process.

Partly due to these difficulties, neighbourhood policing teams and beat managers were invariably given a central role in implementing dispersal orders. In this, CSOs often played a prominent part (where dispersal powers had been conferred upon them by their chief constable). Many CSOs reported that their role in policing dispersal zones gave them a greater sense of authority and status:

'So it provided the CSOs with actually going from being toothless to [a situation in which] they had some teeth…. So, it actually gave the CSOs a little bit of authority.' (Middle-ranking officer, West Yorkshire Police)

While this increase in authority was mostly welcomed by CSOs, the discretionary and contentious nature of the powers might draw them increasingly into adversarial and confrontational situations, a shift that could undermine their relations with young people (Crawford et al, 2005).

Where ASB is prevalent and persistent the policing of dispersal orders generated information about individuals and problems that was usefully linked to other ASB interventions and preventive strategies. Repeated breaches of dispersal directions were used as evidence to support such measures:

> 'If people have been asked to disperse but come back again and again and then again we will be collating that because if that is the case and people are coming back and acting in an unacceptable manner, day after day, then we can use that evidence if we wanted to go, for example, for an anti-social behaviour order.' (Front-line officer, Rotherham)

In this regard, police often worked closely with local authority ASB coordinators with an overview of wider police and partnership responses. Dispersal orders therefore can have a prominent introductory place within a hierarchy of ASB interventions.

An important aspect of implementation entailed consideration of any likely displacement effects generated by a dispersal order. In many dispersal zones the movement of those engaged in ASB to places beyond the boundaries of the designated area was a common occurrence. Consequently, during the pre-authorisation stage several police forces sought to identify potential displacement areas. Armed with such information, strategies were developed to forestall displacement by anticipating where this might occur and targeting additional visible patrols at these areas. This foresight inevitably also had further resource implications.

One concern articulated by several police officers was that a dispersal order, being a police-led enforcement strategy, might be perceived as letting partner agencies 'off the hook'. As the dispersal order often became the centrepiece of what was generally a wider approach, at least in terms of the media and public profile, this could allow key partners to take less active responsibility, by 'leaving it to the police'.

The most frequent analogy used by professionals and lay people to explain the value of a dispersal order was that of a 'sticking plaster' – with a short-term limited use but unable to address the cause of the problem – as the following police officer with experience of three dispersal orders explains:

> 'I think it's a sticking plaster. It gave a lot of respite and sent out a good message to young people that that sort of behaviour would not be tolerated. However, long term there's got to be better solutions. It's something that is very useful in specific areas for specific problems but you can't rely on that alone as solving your problem. There's lots more solutions in respect of involving the schools more, involving parents more, lots of different outreach workers, youth clubs and so on, which are perhaps somewhat beyond our reach. Other organisations have a role to play. Yes, I would say a sticking plaster but a very useful sticking plaster, when times get pretty bad in certain areas.' (Middle-ranking officer, Staffordshire Police)

As this officer implies, the long-term success of any strategy to address ASB must involve a significant element of preventive and diversionary activities, beyond the police remit.

Use of escort powers

In the light of the original Richmond court case,[10] the use of the escort power was suspended by police forces across the country. Even when the Court of Appeal decision overturned the original judgment[11] and new guidance was produced in June 2006, many police forces preferred not to use the power, either as a matter of general policy or within specific applications for dispersal orders. As the data presented earlier in this chapter show, this power has been very little used. Some police officers felt that the power was either unnecessary, counterproductive or obscured the main aims of the dispersal order given its association with curfews:

> 'So was there a need? I question it. Should they have been as naive to believe that "oh, it'll be alright, no one's really going to moan about this"? I think we were naive. What were all the headlines initially when these things came about in 2004? "Police impose curfew on under-16s". Up and down the country that was the headline, left, right and centre, which then detracted from some of the good work we did in trying to bring young people on board, to bring them in to youth provision, to bring them into partnership working with the police and so forth.' (Middle-ranking officer, Metropolitan Police)

One of the implications of politicians' fondness to introduce new legal powers to address social problems, often without full consideration of the impact on other legal mechanisms, is that new powers often overlap with or duplicate existing powers, thus creating uncertainties among practitioners over which powers to use. Some police questioned whether the new escort powers were necessary given available authority to take young people under the age of 18 into police protection, provided by the 1989 Children Act.

Exit strategies

Exit strategies inevitably raise difficult questions for those who have overseen implementation. They present challenges about what, if anything, should replace a dispersal order, while offering opportunities to imprint a legacy. Where partner agencies have been galvanised, the exit strategy was couched among a range of diversionary and preventive measures, renewed forms of civic participation and improvements in local public services or infrastructure. In many instances, however, the exit strategy was predominantly concerned with the challenge of managing the reduction of additional police resources provided for enforcement without disappointing the local community:

> 'And what we're looking at is how we're going to phase out the police officers. We can't go from one day having a lot of police officers up there to the next day having none. So we'll look at phasing that out gradually and reducing the number of police officers gradually over a given period of time.' (Front-line officer, South Yorkshire Police)

Interestingly, the publicity courted at the front end of a dispersal order was rarely replicated at exit. Initiatives tend to be allowed to fade from view, with little information passed to the public that dispersal powers no longer applied. Not only did this fail to relay any assessment of progress (or otherwise) of the dispersal order, it was likely to leave many among the community hesitant as to whether the powers still applied in the designated area, potentially resulting in public uncertainty and disappointment:

---

[10] R. (W) v Metropolitan Police and the London Borough of Richmond (July, 2005).

[11] R. (on the application of W) v Commissioner of Police of the Metropolis (May, 2006).

'I'm a little bit disappointed because I think it's a missed opportunity for the police in terms of the public profile and the effectiveness or not of that particular mechanism. And I also think the police are doing young people a disservice because it's just petered out, there hasn't been as much publicity about it ending as there was beginning. So I don't actually know what young people out there think. Do they know it's finished?' (Housing officer, North Yorkshire)

In some instances, the lack of publicity signalling the end of a dispersal order was a deliberate strategy. The intention was to avoid sending out a message that might be interpreted as meaning a lessening of police concern for, or interest in, the area or a return to the pre-designation situation. The implication of this strategy, however, was that publicity at the end of a dispersal order was only to be encouraged when a renewal application had been successful.

Renewal

Where a dispersal order has been implemented there is an understandable tendency for it to generate public pressure for renewal. Not only does renewal address the awkward problem (referred to above) of how to ensure that a reversal back to the pre-designation situation is avoided, but it also guarantees a continuation of heightened policing attention. Furthermore, there is a ratcheting effect on public expectations whereby increased security interventions invariably generate demands for further action (Crawford et al, 2003). Consequently, as dispersal orders near the end of their designation period, demands for their continuation have frequently been loud and sustained. This has resulted in many orders being renewed either immediately or shortly after their initial termination. This explains why over a quarter (27%) of all orders are renewals. Some practitioners expressed concern that dispersal orders were being renewed too readily without sufficient review or evidence. It was felt that in some places an historic problem of ASB was being used to justify renewal rather than a rigorous re-examination of the evidence to support renewal.

The spectre of potential renewal with its knock-on implications for police resources was a further headache for police managers considering authorising a dispersal order, particularly given the variety of competing policing demands with which they have to contend. It also reinforced the potential for dispersal orders to raise the threshold of public expectations as to policing ASB in the longer term:

'I would only do them for a maximum of six months. I knew when these orders were coming to the end and the feeling was expressed at the residents' forum meeting: "what are we going to do if we don't get it again?" They were never meant to get it again! It was never going to be there forever. It was publicised right from the start that it was going to be a six months thing and it would only be in very, very exceptional circumstances that you would extend it beyond six months. And I think it would be a major worry for us if we had to extend it after six months, because if you've put that amount of effort into something for six months and it hasn't had the effect, then you're doing something wrong with it really.' (Middle-ranking officer, North Yorkshire Police)

The decision to renew prompts questions concerning judgements about the success of an initiative. Some police and local authority officers explicitly saw renewal as a clear indication of failure. Others, however, argued that where an order had successfully reduced the incidence of ASB, this might be used as evidence to justify the continuation of the order. This view was frequently provoked by fear that terminating the order would allow the situation to deteriorate again. One police officer, frustrated by this short-term thinking commented:

'You've got to come up with long-term solutions. So what is the local youth service doing about this? How are we going to communicate with that group? Do they understand why it's being brought in in the first place? Is there any mediation between the group and the community? And [a police officer] said "No, they are just going to bring it back in again, because it seemed to be successful". But before you can bring it in you have to start back from step one. You need to get a group to look at what works well within the area. What didn't work well? And problem-solve that from a multi-agency point of view, because what will happen is all the agencies will stand back and allow the police to police a dispersal area, because in the short term it's successful.' (Middle-ranking officer, Metropolitan Police)

Terminating an order before it has run its full course was widely perceived as evidence of success.

4

A tale of two cities

This chapter reports on the experiences of implementing dispersal orders in two large English cities: Sheffield and Leeds. Here, we take the city as a wider focus of analysis to explore distributional and spatial issues that are less apparent in the narrower analysis of specific case studies (Chapter 5). It also considers specific lessons learnt about the implementation of dispersal orders and developments of strategy over time to assess the longer-term implications and effectiveness of orders that had been implemented some years earlier. It draws on quantitative data and interviews with police and local authority personnel, key local stakeholders and limited observations of police enforcement.

The use of dispersal orders in Sheffield

The experience of Sheffield largely demonstrates the evolution of a very specific implementation strategy towards dispersal orders. Since their introduction, the use of dispersal orders has become increasingly focused on addressing a particular set of problems associated with Halloween and Bonfire night. Dispersal orders have become a central strategy within Operation 'Mischief', a South Yorkshire-wide initiative aimed at providing an annual multi-agency response to ASB, including firework and alcohol misuse. The initiative also serves to provide reassurance for neighbourhoods at what is considered to be a traditionally difficult time of year when large groups of youth congregate and there are heightened instances of ASB.

Over the last three years, the use of dispersal orders has become more focused and targeted in terms of location, duration and implementation strategy (Figure 8). The Sheffield experience was influenced by an early case, arising from events in October 2004, the first year of Operation Mischief, and taken against South Yorkshire Police. In that case a young woman had her conviction for breaching a dispersal order quashed on the basis

Figure 8: Number of dispersal orders across Sheffield, by year

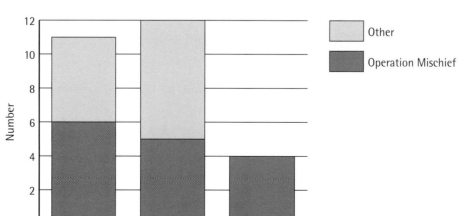

that the authorisation failed adequately to explain the grounds on which it was based.[12] This proved a hard but important lesson in ensuring a rigorous authorisation process and clarity over the grounds for, and purpose of, future dispersal orders.

Dispersal orders have been used in areas where firework misuse has been problematic and in some cases where this has been linked to racially motivated behaviour. In 2006, the operation lasted three-and-a-half weeks, covering the period immediately before and after Halloween, Mischief night and Bonfire night.[13] Four areas of the city were the subject of dispersal orders, all of which had previously been the subject of a dispersal order. By contrast, in 2004 six areas had authorised dispersal zones. On the basis of the analysis intelligence from the previous year, the size of the dispersal zones was reduced in all but one of the areas in 2006. The experience of previous years has allowed the police, in consultation with others, to narrow the focus and sharpen the objectives of the operation. In 2006, dispersal orders in Sheffield were only being used in the context of Operation Mischief (its third year of operation).

Authorisation process

There are benefits that accrue from the process of authorisation when rigorously implemented and based on local information about ASB-related problems and the focused nature of the response to them. A police officer noted:

> 'My general thoughts are it's a useful power to have. It's a power that we can invoke by going through a process, and showing that we require to invoke that power to prevent nuisance disorder, anti-social behaviour, in a specific location, through a specific period of time.' (Middle-ranking police officer)

There are at least three direct process benefits. The first derives from the process of analysing the nature of the problem and considering both multi-agency and community-based responses. It allows for a taking stock of the evidence and a strategic approach to potential problem-solving of which Section 30 power may only play a small part. The second derives from engaging with the community to provoke a debate about appropriate use of public space. The third benefit lies in the accountability that derives from a rigorous analysis of the nature of the problems and dialogue about how these might best be addressed. It requires the police and local authority to account in advance for a particular policing strategy in a given area. In many senses, this kind of openness and prospective accounting is rare in contemporary policing where accountability largely takes the form of post hoc explanations of actions after the event. In large part, it reflects the exceptional nature of the powers and the significant restrictions on individuals' liberty they permit.

Implementation

During the authorisation period in 2006 some 936 patrol hours were dedicated to the four targeted areas drawing on a total of 77 officers. This represents a slight increase on the number of patrol hours over the previous year (Table 2), despite the narrowing of the geographic boundaries of most of the areas. This high level of police involvement and activity reflects the resource-intensive nature of the implementation strategy. In Sheffield it was acknowledged that meeting community expectations demanded significant levels of visible policing:

---

[12] Sierny V The Director of Public Prosecutions [2006] EWHC 716.

[13] Mischief night is a particular Yorkshire variant of Halloween, which falls on the night before bonfire night – 4 November – rather than on 30 October.

Table 2: Operation Mischief (Sheffield) police performance data (2005–06)

	2005	2006	% change 2005–06
Stop Forms completed	168	155	−8
Arrested for ASB	17	14	−18
Number of PNDs	5	13	+160
National Intelligence Report forms completed	29	7	−76
Officers deployed	96	77	−20
Hours patrolling hotspots	627	936	+49

'If we weren't prepared to put in the staff to police a Section 30 order properly, then there is not much point in us putting it on in the first place – if we haven't got the staff to respond to the calls.' (Middle-ranking police officer)

In all, 155 formal stops were made (resulting in the completion of a Stop Form). Some 14 people were arrested for ASB-related incidents and 13 penalty notices for disorder (PNDs) were issued. As Table 2 shows, this represents a reduction in the numbers stopped and arrested compared to the previous year but also indicates a greater use of PNDs (only available for those 16 years and older). It also reinforces the light touch implementation strategy preferred.

The strategy adopted by the police was to operate in the shadow of dispersal powers and use them to engage in informal discussions with young people about acceptable behaviour and what the police might do if there are reports of ASB:

'I think in some cases just speaking to people and saying: "are you aware of the dispersal order?"; "be aware that the police and the public are watching your behaviour"; and "we will ask you to go home or remove you to your home if you are behaving anti-socially" [is sufficient] ... I think it is policed very sensibly, sensitively and certainly not as a carpet power to clear the streets on an evening. I think we target it in the right locations based on the analysis that the previous years have given us.' (Middle-ranking police officer)

It was decided that young people under 16 out after 9pm in the targeted areas would be spoken to but not escorted home. The police, city council and partner agencies all agreed that dispersal orders should be used not as a stand-alone measure to address a problem in the short term. Rather they were to be used in conjunction with a variety of measures as a part of a long-term and sustainable multi-agency approach. Hence, dispersal orders were part of a larger policing initiative including the following:

- there was a Police and Trading Standards crackdown on the illegal selling (and buying) of fireworks and alcohol;
- a public firework display was organised by the council;
- youth services provided extra diversionary activities and opened a youth club.
- the fire service sought to inform youths and residents of the dangers associated with fireworks;
- there were truancy sweeps during the daytime;
- police made visits to schools in and near the targeted areas to explain the dangers of fireworks, acceptable behaviour and the role of the dispersal order.

A city council officer reinforced both the limited role of enforcement and the importance of alternative diversionary activities:

'The main point around the Section 30 is that you are asking people not to be on the streets in groups if they appear to be causing nuisance. We wanted to make sure that they had something else to do … we've been quite careful that we didn't just [remove] people … giving people the impression that they weren't allowed to be hanging around on the streets without anything else for them to do, young people especially. The Section 30 wasn't going to solve the problem of the anti-social behaviour; it was just a means of providing respite for residents.'

In a related vein, a police officer emphasised the need to link the short-term nature of the dispersal orders into a longer-term strategy:

'Let's look at what prevention we can put in place, to prevent that disorder from occurring without invoking a Section 30. Let's have the Section 30 in our back pocket if you like, if we can't resolve the matters elsewhere. If we can't, then let's put it on the table and use the dispersal order. Let's resolve the situation in the short term, and then have another look at how we can perhaps resolve it in the longer term, so that we're not going through the same situation again in six or twelve months time. So it's a useful power to have, almost as a fall-back position, when we know through analysis that previous interventions have failed.' (Middle-ranking police officer)

Measuring success

In 2004, the first year that dispersal orders were used within Operation Mischief, firework-related incidents across South Yorkshire fell by 7%, as compared to the same period of time the previous year. Larger falls were reported in the Sheffield Central policing area where such incidents declined by 28% and malicious incidents by 43%. The Fire Service reported similar benefits with the total number of incidents across the Sheffield district declining on the previous year by 30%, with the number of secondary fires falling by 45%. Ambulance Service data show a reduction in the number of firework-related injuries over the three years from 24 in 2004 to 13 in 2005 and seven in 2006, less than a third of the number two years earlier. Further, there appears not to have been any significant displacement of firework-related ASB to other parts of the city.

The multi-pronged nature of most interventions left it difficult to determine simple cause and effect relationships in assessing impact. Nevertheless, the high media and public profile accorded to the dispersal powers, even where not enforced strictly, inevitably drew the most attention. This is frequently so, even if, as the police officer quoted above testifies, these powers largely remain 'in the back pocket'. Furthermore, the perceived success of the dispersal orders has created something of a dilemma in as much as it has fuelled demands to renew orders. For instance, there was some debate about whether dispersal orders were genuinely needed as part of Operation Mischief in 2006 given the progress of the two previous years. Eventually, it was felt that the problem had not been fully resolved and, perhaps more importantly for some, there was a need to 'keep the pressure up'. A city council officer alluded to the tensions caused by apparent success:

'Broadly speaking the community has been extremely supportive. It's generated even more support as they've been seen to be successful to the extent that I think we're kind of holding back on them now because they've been very successful. But I think people were starting to get a bit, not reliant on them but they were seen to be so successful and I think people were starting to say we want one in our area. And we were saying: "well yes, they have worked in the past but actually they don't solve all the problems". We'd rather solve the problems than just put the Section 30 in for a short period of time that just ends.'

Despite this assertion, in 2007 plans were in place to extend the duration of the dispersal orders in the four areas previously covered to five months, to incorporate the summer months as well as the Halloween and Bonfire period.

The Leeds experience

Since becoming available in early 2004, 13 dispersal orders have been introduced within the city of Leeds. These have been used by the police mostly in a trouble-shooting capacity, in reaction to the emergence of group-related ASB and in response to local councillors' and residents' demands for police action. In the first two years, 10 dispersal orders were authorised, often in an experimental capacity. By contrast, in 2006, only two areas were designated as dispersal zones and this same pattern continued in the first half of 2007 when only one new dispersal order was authorised (see Figure 9). This significant reduction in use is largely attributable to concerns of police managers that dispersal orders are resource intensive to enforce, short term in outlook and narrow in focus, and can strain relations between young people and the police, as well as between different communities.

Figure 9: Number of dispersal orders across Leeds, by year

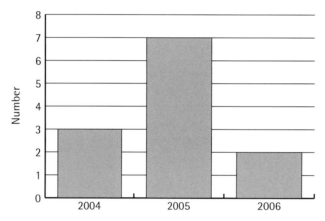

The city centre has been the focus of three dispersal orders, each of six months in duration. One quarter of all orders have been renewals, slightly lower than the national figures and those for London (see Chapter 3). The average length of orders has been just under five months, with most designated for six months and a smaller number for three months (Figure 10).

Figure 10: Duration of dispersal orders across Leeds (2004–06)

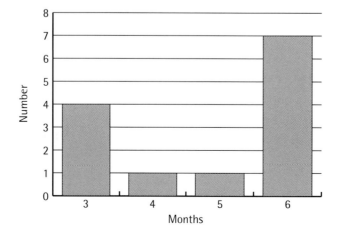

City-wide distribution

Across Leeds, dispersal orders have also been used in a variety of residential areas. Three quarters of all dispersal orders issued by the end of 2006 were located in only one of three police divisions covering Leeds and its environs. Significantly, no straightforward threshold of ASB exists, above which a dispersal order is triggered. Consequently, some areas that experience high levels of crime and disorder have not yet been the subject of a dispersal order.

The distribution of dispersal orders across the city has been shaped by a range of factors in addition to the level and concentration of crime and ASB. This includes the commitment of local politicians and police managers, the pressures to which they are subject, as well as the capacity of local communities and groups to voice their concerns over ASB and have them acted on by relevant authorities. Elected councillors can play a major role in pressurising the police to use available new powers without necessarily understanding fully the implications:

> 'Local politicians are aware of all the new powers under the Crime and Disorder Act and are really, really quite keen. They see these as solutions to problems, where often we see them as a short-term control measure.' (Police manager)

Furthermore, the role of senior police officers in authorising and championing the use of dispersal orders is not only a formal aspect of the authorisation process but also reflects personal preferences:

> 'Dispersal orders can sometimes be influenced by personalities. You've got an inspector who's particularly, "let's get it in place, it's another enforcement tool and we can crack down hard on these yobs". Then it's more likely to be pushed forwards.' (Local authority representative)

A learning process

Across the city a more considered view has developed within the police regarding the appropriate value of dispersal orders, as indicated by the reduced usage. This reflects a degree of organisational learning among those agencies involved in the authorisation, implementation and enforcement of the orders. As in Sheffield, there was a widespread acknowledgement that dispersal orders should be introduced alongside a range of diversionary interventions delivered and funded through partnership structures. Recently, there has been a preference for orders of less than six months. This allows for review and assessment of the order after the initial period of intensive enforcement, which is a recurring feature of dispersal orders. Thereafter, if considered beneficial, the dispersal order can be extended. The lessons learnt suggest that dispersal orders are better used with caution and should remain in place for no longer than necessary. Short orders send out clearer signals regarding the exceptional nature of the powers and the need for longer-term strategic planning to address the issues that have provoked their introduction:

> 'We said that we would only do it for three months. The reason was we wanted to explain and exaggerate [to the community] that it's just a short-term measure. This is not the long-term strategy. We'll use it and we think it will be effective but we need other things in place to change this area for the medium and the longer term.' (Police manager)

The initial dispersal orders were six-month initiatives and predominantly enforcement-led. Although these gained short-term reductions in ASB, they were accompanied by some displacement problems. For instance, one dispersal order had detrimental consequences for a youth centre in a neighbouring area. As youths who were displaced from the dispersal zone began attending the centre, its activities became disrupted and, allegedly as a consequence of a resulting exclusion policy, the building was set on fire.

This served as a reminder that the use of dispersal orders needed to be more problem-solving in approach and partnership-led. Several subsequent dispersal orders have stimulated crime prevention activity in conjunction with other agencies and prompted partner organisations to consider what they might do to address the broader conditions that underpin ASB. Senior police officers recognised the role that dispersal orders can play, as exceptional measures, in persuading partner agencies to contribute to a joined-up approach to local problems:

> 'I think the dispersal order is good because the police [can] say: "we'll only use it if...!" And that way it can be used to lever other agencies. "We'll only use this if you provide extra youth provision." And so it can be used as a leverage tool to galvanise other agencies into taking some business.' (Police manager)

Early engagement with other local agencies and pre-implementation planning enabled various diversionary local activities to be established in conjunction with one dispersal order, including educational support, youth services and other forms of community provision. The local partnership was able to use the dispersal order as a catalyst to form a residents' group to help support its activities aimed at tackling ASB, as well as to lever in external funding:

> 'We contacted a number of other statutory agencies so there was education, youth services, social services, housing, the police, and we all sat round the table and we came up with an action plan of which a number of services were all going to contribute different things.' (Middle-ranking police officer)

Part of this funding supported outreach workers who began a dialogue with young people about acceptable norms of behaviour. It also sponsored diversionary youth activities. Equally, local schools provided a forum for discussion about ASB with input from local police officers. In so doing, the partnership successfully dovetailed enforcement and diversionary goals. For example, the police and youth services established a joint database to allow information sharing, such that the latter undertook preventive follow-up visits to individuals who had been dispersed. Police action alone was seen as inadequate in addressing the root causes of ASB, as the following senior police officer acknowledged:

> 'Dispersal orders on their own are not an answer. And I won't even engage in one now unless I know up front what the "buy-in" is from relevant partners because, in terms of enforcement there's quite a big investment by police. But I know that unless other people buy into it and provide longer-term problem-solving, in six months of relative calm, it won't make any difference long-term.' (Police manager)

As well as recognising the limitations of enforcing dispersal orders in isolation of more supportive measures, officers overseeing their implementation have become aware of their tendency to raise expectations among the community. To address this, early consultation with the community is seen as crucial if expectations about the likely role and impact of dispersal orders are to be kept in reasonable check. As the following police officer suggests, consultation is also necessary given the powers are exceptional and discretionary:

> 'There's got to be some community consultation. I think it is quite intrusive and restrictive, and as a piece of legislation [it] should be used thoughtfully, properly

and appropriately. So, for that element you need consultation.' (Middle-ranking police officer)

The slowdown in the use of dispersal orders across Leeds reflects the view within the city that they should be used sparingly, as an integrated response within a wider raft of partnership activities.

Designating the size and focus

Across the city, dispersal areas have varied in size and focus. Those that have focused on highly localised vicinities (for example outside a parade of shops or recreational facility) tend to have experienced greater problems of displacement, as it is easier for those dispersed to regroup in nearby areas. For this reason, a dispersal order introduced in 2006 arising from concerns about the congregation of youths known as 'moshers' around a shopping arcade in the city centre was expanded to incorporate much of the commercial area of the city centre. As a result of consultation prior to the application process, in which concerns about displacement were voiced and other ASB-related issues came to light, the boundaries of the order were considerably expanded to include, for example, a large hospital on the edge of the city centre. This demonstrates how the need to consult can create pressures to expand the size and focus of dispersal zones. As more organisations are drawn into the consultation process, wider concerns over ASB may come to light. In addition, possible displacement effects from a proposed dispersal order can give rise to demands to incorporate neighbouring areas within a designated dispersal zone. The subjective definition of ASB adds to this pressure. It can lead to dispersal orders embracing multiple aims and blurring goals. The expansionist logic runs contrary to the manageability and effectiveness of small-scale and sharply focused dispersal orders.

The larger the dispersal zone, the more difficult it becomes to keep out those who engage in ASB – this can raise challenges when those engaging in ASB are 'insiders', living within the dispersal area. Where those dispersed live within the designated zone, uncertainties arise as to the directions police are able to give, partly as they cannot exclude residents from the area. This issue was compounded by reservations over police powers to escort children under 16 home.

Within a dispersal order that covered several communitys in the semi-rural area, officers decided it was inappropriate to disperse young people out of the dispersal zone. Instead, they chose to move groups to places within the designated area where they would be less likely to be seen to be causing a nuisance:

'So officers on the street and PCSOs were able to ask them to go elsewhere and go to a play area, somewhere away from the housing where they were causing the problems, and it worked.' (Middle-ranking police officer)

Enforcement through additional police resources

A consistent policy in Leeds has been to enforce dispersal orders intensively as soon as they become operational, predominantly through additional high-visibility patrols. This strategy is designed to make a considerable impact from the outset. However, it risks raising public expectations over suitable levels of police visibility and is difficult for police managers to sustain over a period of time. Consequently, local police managers stressed the importance of an enforcement strategy detailing the planned deployment of resources over the duration of the dispersal order:

'Because what happens with a dispersal order is you do a lot of press, you put in extra resources to try and have an impact, but you can't maintain them. So, you can get a quick fix but it's not necessarily a long-term gain, unless you put in resources and manage to keep them there.' (Police manager)

Few dispersal orders in the city have been able to maintain the initial level of resources, albeit one division was able to circumvent this problem by levering partnership money to fund additional patrols.

The desire to 'hit an area hard and early' frequently also jeopardises the extent to which a dispersal order can be solely enforced by deploying locally based neighbourhood teams whose members have greater knowledge of, and familiarity with the local area: its people, places and problems. Most neighbourhood policing teams are insufficiently resourced to sustain increased levels of police visibility. As a consequence, officers who may lack extensive local knowledge have tended to be brought into an area to help resource the initial enforcement period. In so doing, there is a risk that these officers may perceive their policing role to be narrow and coercively orientated:

'You're buying in officers who, with the best will in the world, are aware of the powers but the application of those powers to that particular community is a very blunt instrument ... there is this potential for conflict if it's enforced by people who don't know the local area.' (Police manager)

This view outlines the potential for the inappropriate or inconsistent use of dispersal powers by officers who are unfamiliar with the local context.

Enforcement support through housing controls

A dispersal order in one area of the city demonstrated the importance of incorporating housing management organisations into the enforcement strategy. It had been hoped to combine dispersal orders with tenancy controls, by using 'repeat dispersals' as evidence that those engaged in persistent ASB were breaking their tenancy obligations. However, as the majority of the local housing stock in the area was owned and managed by private (often absentee) landlords, police were mostly unable to gain the necessary cooperation, given the fragmented nature of the landlords' interests. Hence, they were not able to use the dispersal order as intended in conjunction with threats concerning eviction proceedings. By contrast, it was often noted to be much easier for police to work with social housing providers and estate management organisations, which tend to have a far greater stake in, and ownership over, community problems.

Impact over time

The experience above outlines the potential pitfalls of using a dispersal order in high crime areas, when a less confrontational approach might be more beneficial. Here, a small group of seemingly determined youths taunted the police and, having quickly learnt the 'rules' of the dispersal order, engaged them in a game of 'cat and mouse', which resulted in recorded levels of ASB increasing. As the main protagonists were displaced into less visible spaces, they were able to commit criminal damage more discreetly and without challenge from the police or local residents:

'When we got them out of the main area, the main shops and the main roads, they were actually removed into the ginnels[14] where they could cause more damage.... And so I got battered on my criminal damage figures, absolutely battered.' (Middle-ranking police officer)

This demonstrates the potential for dispersal orders to harden antagonistic attitudes between young people and police. It suggests that dispersal orders may be less suitable for those particularly marginalised estates where criminality and ASB are often deeply engrained:

'They're probably effective in better-to-do areas with lesser and lower levels of criminality, residential areas. We tried it in an area which really, some of them [youth] were well beyond hope, what we actually gave them was a bit more of a sense of purpose and unity.' (Middle-ranking police officer)

Although several dispersal orders implemented across the city are reported to have led to short-term reductions of ASB, they are widely viewed as being less successful in effecting sustainable change. Locally, dispersal orders have been used by the police to gain a short-term grip on an area, which is then supplemented by the introduction of partnership crime prevention activities:

'So my experience is, yes, they're an effective tool for the short-term issues and they sort the short-term problem out. There's also a sense that it doesn't alter their behaviour, it just moves them across the street. And so it doesn't actually address the disease, it's just a sticking plaster.' (Police manager)

As described, the enforcement of the dispersal order usually generated short-term increases in police visibility within the designated area. Unsurprisingly, one recurring consequence has been for residents to ask for its continuation as a means of capturing a scarce public resource, namely visible police patrols. For the police, this positive community response was tempered by the difficulties of sustaining the increased level of policing:

'We can only sustain this for a three-month period. We're going to have to find different ways of dealing with problems in this area other than throwing police resources at it, which is always a quick fix.' (Police manager)

One officer who oversaw a dispersal order was subsequently reticent about reusing the powers because he felt that it had served to lower adult residents' tolerance of young people and their behaviour. This led to deterioration in relations between young people, the local community and police. Several officers having overseen the implementation of dispersal orders offered similar warnings:

'I don't want to alienate the youth. And at the end of the day, they are quite stringent powers placing restrictions on people. You've got to be very careful about causing that divide, very careful about how you police these youngsters, how you engage with them. And make sure that you don't [marginalise them]. Make them feel they're full members of the community and their rights are just as important as other people's.' (Middle-ranking police officer)

The beneficial side-effects of dispersal orders often reside in the enhanced level of community dialogue and enduring partnership activity that they can stimulate. In some areas, the introduction of a dispersal order led to formal meetings and prompted discussions between different community interests about appropriate behaviour and

---

[14] Ginnels are narrow alleyways that usually run between two rows of terraced housing.

facilities for young people. In some instances, this has involved young people who have been encouraged to articulate their concerns. Nevertheless, there was evidence of a growing concern among some practitioners of the symbolic messages that dispersal orders communicate, notably to young people.

Conflict with youth

Police recognised that dispersal orders could bring increased conflict between the police and young people. This was particularly apparent among the youths affected by the city centre dispersal orders. One young person articulated the perceived grievances felt by the so-called 'moshers' who had traditionally congregated around a shopping arcade in the city centre:

> 'More trouble will be caused if these youths do not have a place to simply meet and talk. And people will simply find a new meeting place.... In time people will probably decide that we can't congregate there either, and we will be stuck in this eternal game of cat and mouse ... the people that choose to use the area as a meeting point should not be persecuted simply for the way they dress and the lifestyle they choose to follow. This is persecution of the lowest sort, and just because we aren't old enough to vote doesn't mean we should be disregarded and treated as criminals.... This is an infringement of our civil liberties, and we shouldn't stand for it. Being young is not a crime.'

Senior police managers acknowledged that part of the problem was one of managing the appearance of places as conducive to business rather than actual levels of crime and ASB caused by the youths:

> 'A lot of this is around the moshers.... Actually, in terms of their involvement in crime and such, [there are] no issues at all, but they do cause, by their behaviour and the fact that they are gathering in very large groups up and around the [shopping arcade], a great deal of concern for certain groups of people.' (Police manager)

A business owner in the shopping arcade gave a rather different interpretation of the need for the dispersal order:

> 'It's not about youth, it's not about how people look, it's not even necessarily about how individuals behave, it's about the slow death of the [shopping arcade].... The last 15 years has seen a slow succession of owners hiking the rents more and more and have made it even harder for us to survive. This year so far I believe four tenants have gone bust and at least three others are hanging on by the skin of their teeth. Now if you take that situation and plonk any mass group outside the front door that reduce the number of people coming into the centre, it's just going to get worse.' (Business owner)

Another business owner added:

> 'People are just frightened to come in and it's not just older people, it's across the board. It's young people as well, just frightened to come in the building. And obviously now it's got a reputation for itself, people just won't come – full stop. So, it's people like myself who are suffering, and I'm obviously having to lay staff off.'

The fact that large congregations of young people outside a major shopping location can cause obstruction, inconvenience to shoppers, loss of trade and ultimately loss of revenue appears to have been a significant factor in the introduction of the dispersal order. This raises important issues about the signals sent out by the dispersal order about who is welcome within a city centre and who is deemed inappropriate, less because of their behaviour and more because of the way others perceive them. It may be rather incongruous that youths hanging around are dispersed but that groups of revellers who come to spend money in the city's bars and clubs (whose behaviour may well on occasions be anti-social) are courted and welcomed.

5

Two case studies

This chapter presents the findings from two case studies in which dispersal orders were implemented. Supplementing the more general overviews provided by both the national data and experiences and the two city-based studies, the findings provide a more detailed and textured analysis of the micro-social interactions and impacts of dispersal orders within specific localities. Of particular concern was the manner in which dispersal orders were experienced and interpreted by adults and youths, rather than merely those implementing them. Hence, the research focused on residential areas as this would provide populations from whom an assessment of the impact of the orders could be gauged. The areas selected were suburbs of an Outer London borough and a northern city ('Southby' and 'Northston' respectively). The research followed the authorisation and implementation of a six-month dispersal order in each site. It draws on interviews with key local stakeholders, residents, businesses and young people attending a nearby secondary school as well as observation of police enforcement practices in each area. In addition, surveys of adult residents and those attending local schools were conducted shortly after the end of each order to assess their impact.[15]

The case studies are not intended to be representative of all dispersal orders. As our national overview (Chapter 3) demonstrates, dispersal orders have been used in a variety of different types of location, in response to a range of ASB-related problems, and with diverse implementation strategies. One case study area was selected in discussion with the research funders; the other case study site was chosen in consultation with staff at the Central Safer Neighbourhoods Unit in the Metropolitan Police Service. While there is no such thing as a stereotypical dispersal order, the case studies well illustrate the issues raised by their use in certain types of residential areas.

While something of an oversimplification, both areas might be characterised as representing reasonably low crime suburban localities with relatively stable residential populations, hosting a small number of local shops and amenities, in which groups of young people had become associated with ASB and provoked growing complaints from residents and businesses. The strong similarities between the two areas, although largely unintended, allow useful comparisons to be drawn (Table 3).

Both areas also had well-organised forums for voicing residents' concerns, which enabled vocal sections of the community to articulate their grievances and policing preferences.

Northston is neither a high crime area, nor are there high levels of neighbourhood disorder. Nevertheless, it reflects the kind of concerns over perceptions of insecurity that have become commonplace in many parts of Britain. Much of the concern related to the behaviour of groups of 'nuisance youths', congregating in public spaces during the evening. This was often compounded at the weekend, both by underage drinking and the

---

Table 3: Composition of the case study locations

	Northston	Southby
Local shops	✓	✓
Pubs/off-licences	X	✓
Park area	✓	✓
Nearby schools	✓	✓
Public library	✓	✓
CCTV	✓	X
Public transport links	Bus	Bus/underground
Tenure balance	Mostly social renting	Mostly owner occupation

convergence of youths from neighbouring areas. These problems have tended to be highly localised, occurring most acutely in the vicinity of the common amenities – the shops, swimming pool, library and community hall. Consequently, some residents complained of being frequently intimidated when entering these 'communal spaces'.

Over recent years, a variety of initiatives have been supported that have been designed, at least in part, to address adult residents' concerns about ASB and low-level crime. These include:

- part funding a community police officer to provide visible reassurance (2000-02);
- installing CCTV cameras at a number of locations in the community (September 2002);
- introducing private security patrols (2002-05);
- holding a seminar in the community about ASB (October 2004);
- rewarding 'pro-social' behaviour by young people with the aim of encouraging greater tolerance of young people's visible presence (2004-06);
- a dialogue-focused project aimed at addressing intergeneration concerns and misunderstandings (2006-07).

The use of dispersal orders in Northston was first mooted in June 2004, prompted by a local police document entitled *Reclaiming Public Space*. However, the police decided not to advance the initiative as it was felt that the level of crime and ASB did not warrant it. In November 2005, a multi-agency Joint Action Group was formed combining neighbouring communities, to consider ways of tackling a range of local issues, including residents' concerns over ASB. This forum provided a channel for early consultations about possible dispersal order applications that were proposed in two areas in early 2006 after a number of incidents. The applications were to cover the centre of Northston and a specific location in the neighbouring community.

Police data on all ASB incidents for the wider area between 1 October 2005 and 31 January 2006 were sifted and those with clear connections to groups of young people were mapped. This mapping exercise revealed what was considered to be sufficient evidence of persistent ASB and a problem with groups causing intimidation (as required by the legislation) in the neighbouring community, but not of itself in Northston. Consequently, police data in the latter were supplemented by the local social landlord's recorded data on ASB-related complaints as well as public letters of support, mainly from prominent members of local residents' groups. Collectively, this was deemed sufficient to provide the evidence necessary to trigger authorisation.

In March 2006 authorisation was granted for two six-month orders to be implemented simultaneously, commencing on 1 April 2006. The police operation to support both orders came into effect on the same day that the new neighbourhood policing teams were introduced across the city. As a result, a combination of neighbourhood officers, CSOs and response officers drafted in from the city's main police station, was deployed to the area most evenings over the first few weeks of the order. In Northston the dispersal zone was restricted to the central part of the community covering most of the open green spaces, but not including the outlying residential areas. The reasons given for this were, first, that most of the recorded ASB had occurred in the central area and, second, that this would allow the police to disperse young people out of the area to their homes beyond the zone.

The approach to enforcement was to use the powers only as a last resort. The briefing given to police teams declared: 'Although these powers are available, it is preferable to positively influence behaviour in that location, rather than simply displace anti-social behaviour to a previously unaffected nearby location'. Officers were encouraged to use the existence of the order as a vehicle for engaging with groups of youths within the dispersal zone. Hence, dispersal powers were only to be used when initial advice to groups about behaviour was not heeded. The briefing warned officers of the importance of using powers fairly 'to ensure that we do not lose the local public support'. Officers were also told that when they use the powers they must inform the individuals fully why the powers are being used and the consequences of failure to comply with any direction under it and record this conversation for any subsequent evidential purposes. The briefing also cautioned officers to be wary of any displacement effect. A neighbouring area was singled out as 'a likely displacement location for both zones' that 'should be checked periodically'.

Southby is an urban community in an outer borough of London. The wider ward has a population of 9,993 people (2001 Census) and one of the lowest crime rates in the borough. Like Northston, it has a significant population of older people and a high level of fear of crime. The population is predominantly White (90%). Three pubs are located in close proximity to each other in the centre of Southby and attract groups of young people. There are also off-licence premises in the shopping parade and a history of complaints of underage drinking. There are three schools in the area attended by pupils from across the borough. Behaviour of pupils in the vicinity of the schools had been a source of complaint.

The centre of Southby had been the subject of an earlier dispersal order in 2005, albeit covering a slightly larger area. The earlier order arose, in part, in response to concerns about displacement from the policing of a dispersal order in a neighbouring area. The dispersal order in 2006 was prompted by a survey of residents, which identified youth-related ASB as the most pressing local issue. One of the explicit grounds for the authorisation of the dispersal order related to problems with groups of young people outside the pubs. A further ground was groups of youths committing general forms of ASB. Southby is well served by public transport, making it easily accessible to visitors, and the ability for all under 18-year-olds in education to travel free on buses (with an Oyster Card) was cited by some people (residents and police) as having an impact. The dispersal zone was confined largely to the streets immediately feeding off the central area and, as such, was narrower than the previous order, which had included a number of outlying roads.

Table 4 provides a timeline of key events in the two case studies.

Wider developments

Wider multi-agency initiatives were triggered in both case study areas. The origins of some pre-dated the introduction of the dispersal order. For example, the dialogue project in Northston was born of the earlier seminar and represented an attempt to address sources of intergenerational conflict and misunderstanding, by working with groups of young people and adult residents to explore mutual perceptions and ways in which community members might play more active roles in fostering good relations. During the dispersal

Table 4: Timeline of case studies

	Northston	Southby
January 2006	Police together with local social landlord begin to collect information and data to support an application for a dispersal order	
February 2006	Dialogue project begins, focused on addressing intergenerational conflict Local library changes its hours such that it is closed after school finishes	Neighbourhood Policing introduced to the borough Police Consultative Group vote ASB the most important priority
March 2006	Police Consultative Committee decides to support the dispersal order application Applications from police for two dispersal orders are authorised by local authority	
April 2006	Dispersal powers come into effect Neighbourhood Policing Teams introduced across the city Police officer arranges open meeting to counter possible misunderstandings among parents and young people about the order, but none attend A bus shelter in the centre of the community renowned for youths congregating and vandalism is demolished	
June 2006		The local ASB forum meets to discuss rise in complaints in two streets close to the secondary school
July 2006		Increasing complaints to police about ASB in the main high street and surrounding areas Dispersal order applied for, authorised and publicised
August 2006	Escort powers are activated and residents notified through a local newsletter delivered to all households	Dispersal powers come into effect
October 2006	Dispersal order ends	Reduction in ASB over Halloween period linked to the dispersal order
November 2006	Commitment made to use the library building as a dedicated youth facility, once the contents are relocated to the local school (anticipated for September 2007)	
December 2006		Council funding sought for diversion activities provided by youth service and local theatre group Mosquito ultrasonic device to repel teenagers is installed above a local shop
January 2007		A residential area outside the dispersal zone is identified for additional police patrols after persistent graffiti
February 2007		Dispersal order ends Initial proposal to renew is shelved due to a decline in groups congregating in the area Safer Neighbourhoods Unit promises 18 extra CSOs to combat juvenile crime on bus/school routes
July 2007		A dispersal order in neighbouring area of the borough is re-authorised

period, project workers sought to exploit the community interest and attention generated by the dispersal designation to provoke a wider debate about appropriate behaviour and relations between older and younger people.

In Southby diversionary youth initiatives included a project organised between the police and fire brigade and a local theatre project in conjunction with youth services. Both were secured with external funding. The theatre project was not in operation during the designated period but was due to commence in the summer of 2007. Funding was also being sought to provide organised football through a scheme already in existence in other London boroughs.

In both areas, by contrast, a number of developments occurred that reinforced the image of youth as problematic. In Northston, after complaints about rowdy behaviour by young people in and around the local library, a decision was taken to change its opening hours such that it was no longer open after school hours. Many young people interpreted this as a deliberate attempt to exclude them from the library. In addition, the same month that the dispersal order commenced, a symbolic landmark where groups of youths often congregated – the covered bus shelter in the heart of the community – was demolished. The bus shelter had been repeatedly vandalised and was the subject of much local complaint. Its removal was a further reminder of the lack of places for young people to gather, as was the fact that young people generally felt unwelcome in most of the community's common facilities (notably the community hall).

During the dispersal order, in Southby, an ultrasonic device, known as the 'Mosquito', was attached to a shop in the centre of the community. The device emits high-frequency screeching sounds that carry over a distance of roughly 20 metres, which are audible only to those under about 20 years of age.[16] For many young people this constituted a further indiscriminate (and impersonal) mechanism to disperse all young people regardless of their motivation or behaviour.

Police implementation

In both locations police intended to make an early impact through high-visibility patrols. Throughout, fortnightly updates were prepared for police managers to provide feedback and justify continued allocation of resources. Home visits to youths whose names had been recorded as having been dispersed or warned were also conducted.

Northston

The police operation covering the two dispersal orders in Northston and its neighbouring community provided a total of 548 patrol hours. Figure 11 shows that the orders were most intensively policed during the first six weeks. Thereafter the level of patrol generally declined followed by renewed activity during August. Where the data were disaggregated they suggest that about 40% of patrol time was dedicated to Northston dispersal order and 60% to the neighbouring dispersal zone.

Figure 12 provides an overview of police activities in the Northston dispersal zone. The data should be treated with some caution. As some days police returns were not provided or only partially completed, the data are indicative and constitute a minima rather than a

---

[16] Developed by its inventor in Merthyr Tydfil, the Mosquito is now marketed through a company called Compound Security Systems. It claims to have sold over 3,500 units across the UK in the first year of sales (see www.compoundsecurity.co.uk).

Figure 11: Number of patrol hours[a]

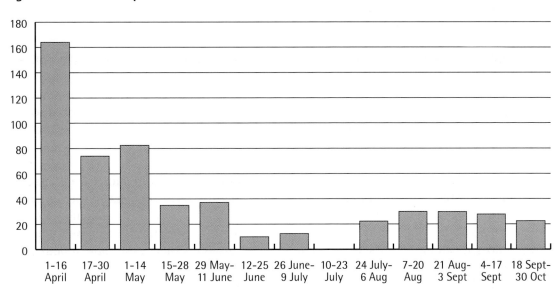

Note: [a]Each column relates to a two-week period except the first (16 days) and the last (covering six weeks).

full reflection of activity. No data for the first 16 days are included as the data collection systems were not in place during that period (which was undoubtedly one of significant activity, as Figure 11 suggests).

Police officers were instructed to complete a Youth Action Form for each encounter they had with a young person. The forms were collated across the city to identify young people at risk of offending and thus facilitate early or other forms of intervention, for example acceptable behaviour contracts. Excluding the first 16 days for which the data were unavailable, at least 21 groups were dispersed during the order, a further 18 groups were formally advised about the dispersal orders and eight offences were dealt with.

Figure 12: Police activity data for Northston

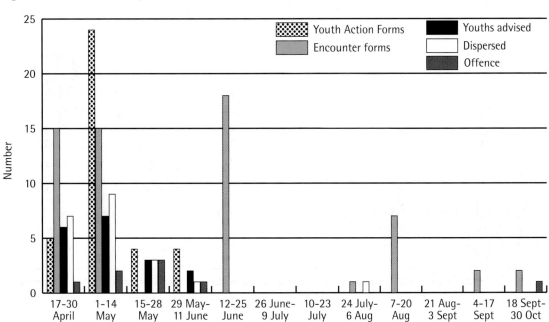

In the neighbouring dispersal zone, by contrast, 42 groups were dispersed and 71 groups were formally advised of the dispersal powers.[17] A total of 18 offences were dealt with during the period, but these were not necessarily non-compliance with the order to disperse.

Observational data collected over five evenings (between 7.30pm and 10.30pm) in both areas confirm the manner in which dispersal powers were implemented. In total, 27 police encounters with groups of young people were observed. Approximately half of these groups were all male, with two being exclusively female. Most groups spoken to included local residents from one or other of the dispersal areas. Most had congregated or were 'hanging around' at the time of the encounter, but a small number were either engaged in playing a game or on the move. In half of the encounters the police entered into a discussion with the young people without directly mentioning the dispersal order or its associated powers. In one third of encounters the police explained the dispersal order and the detrimental consequences of ASB for the community. Four of the 27 encounters (15%) resulted in groups formally being dispersed. On some of these occasions, the names and addresses of those dispersed were neither requested nor recorded. On one occasion, the group was so large that only some names and addresses were taken. On another, a second warning was given for failure to comply with an initial request to disperse. However, none of the incidents resulted in an arrest during the periods of observation.

Observational data and interviews with police confirm that dispersal powers were used flexibly in that 'informal' dispersals often arose, which did not prompt the full activation of the powers, nor the relevant recording process that this entailed. Consequently, young people were often uncertain whether they had been dispersed or simply informed of the existence of the powers. The observational data also highlight the inconsistency of police recording practices.

Southby

In Southby the dispersal order was policed by the Neighbourhood Policing Team of six officers (referred to in London as Safer Neighbourhood Teams), with no significant additional resources. Local police response teams were also briefed about the dispersal order and the enforcement policy. A mobile CCTV van and some special constables were also used on occasions to support the Neighbourhood Policing Team.

Concern was expressed that local residents probably did not realise that significant new police resources were not directly attached to the dispersal order and, hence, managing public expectations was identified from the outset as a crucial concern for the police. Concerns about raising expectation may explain the muted publicity associated with the order. On a visit to the area a few days after the commencement of the order there were no visible signs of the existence of the order. The low level of publicity may explain the relatively small percentage of residents who were aware of the dispersal order (see below).

As in Northston, the police were directed to use their dispersal powers as a tool of last resort and to engage with young people. An important part of the implementation strategy was to target any known offenders and to collect information on groups of young people persistently dispersed. These young people were referred to the Positive Action for Young People (PAYP) scheme run by the council.[18] During the dispersal order five young people

---

[17] Again, data were unavailable for the first 16 days and some entries were incomplete.

[18] The PAYP scheme aims to provide young people at risk with support, guidance and opportunities to undertake positive activities to avoid offending and succeed in education, training or employment.

were referred to the programme. Home visits were also conducted to inform parents about their children's behaviour or involvement with groups. Throughout the period, 105 dispersal warnings were given. Only one youth was escorted home. No arrests were made for anyone breaching a direction to disperse or returning to the area during their period of exclusion.

In line with the implementation of Safer Neighbourhood Teams, a 'ward panel' was in the process of being established during the designation period to act as a channel of communication, consultation and accountability between the police and local community. Ward panels were also being introduced to serve as a vehicle for responding to, and dealing with, local complaints triggered under the 'community calls for action' (introduced by the 2004 Police and Justice Act). During designation, local police were keen to involve a youth representative in the work of the ward panel. A female youth who had been involved in significant ASB but who had subsequently developed good relations with the local police was identified as a potential member of the panel to bring the perspective of young people to deliberations. It was hoped that by involving her 'in part of the solution' rather than seeing her and other young people only 'as part of the problem', it would provide a more constructive way of addressing young people's concerns and listening to their views. Despite these intentions, ultimately it was decided not to invite her to become a member of the ward panel because she was deemed to be 'too young'. Instead she was given a more informal role of informing the local councillor of young people's perspectives and concerns.

Impact on perceptions of residents

There was substantial evidence from observations, interviews and surveys of a decline in the number of young people who congregated in the dispersal zones during the designation. There was also some evidence to suggest that this persisted for at least some time after the end of the dispersal order. As the orders finished during the autumn or winter months it was difficult to know to what extent this was attributable to the weather and seasonal effects. Some residents reported feeling more confident about going out in the area. This decline in the visible presence of groups of youths, of itself, did not necessarily correspond with reduced ASB.

The surveys of adult residents showed that at least half in both areas believed that the order had impacted on the level of young people congregating in the area (Figure 13). Approximately half also felt that it had increased perceptions of safety.

Residents believed that the order was less effective at realising some of the wider potential benefits (Figure 14). Approximately two fifths thought that the order was at least slightly effective at encouraging people to report ASB. However, only about one in six thought that it was effective in encouraging greater respect among the young. In Northston, half (51%) thought it was either 'not very effective' or 'not at all effective' in this regard.

Northston residents appeared to have detected a more favourable impact of the dispersal order and related initiatives compared to Southby. The only exception to this concerned improving police response to complaints of ASB where just under a third of residents in both areas suggested that the order had had some beneficial effect.

Figure 13: Residents' views on effectiveness of dispersal order on crime and ASB (% at least 'slightly effective')

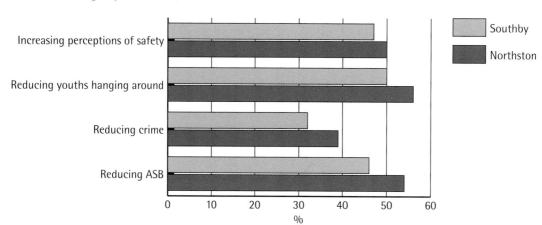

Figure 14: Residents' views of effectiveness on wider benefits (% at least 'slightly effective')

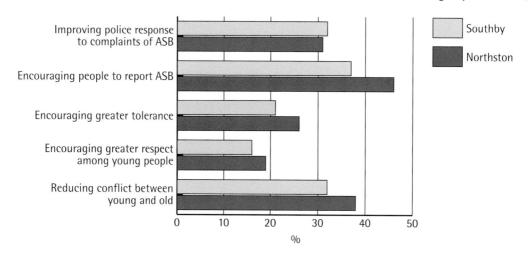

Impact on crime and ASB

One important indicator of the impact of dispersal orders may be provided by police data on recorded crime and calls regarding ASB. Before considering these data the following caveats apply to the veracity of the data and the integrity of drawing causal conclusions:

- The data presented relate to incidents recorded by the police, and hence suffer from both reporting and recording shortfalls, as highlighted by the British Crime Surveys.
- There are considerable fallibilities in the geo-coding of the location of crime incidents and ASB reports to the police.
- The tight geographic focus of the data presented and the relatively infrequent occurrence of incidents of crime and ASB in each of the areas mean that a certain degree of 'natural' or 'random' fluctuation is inevitable. Given the small number of incidents any changes may appear to be considerable.
- It is problematic to attribute changes in recorded crime directly to the introduction of dispersal orders. There may be many factors influencing fluctuations.

Northston

Figure 15 shows the levels of recorded crime aggregated into six-month periods that correspond with the dates of the dispersal order (1 April to 30 September 2006). In Northston crime decreased both in comparison with the preceding six months (39%) and the same period the previous year (19%).

Figure 15: Recorded crime in Northston

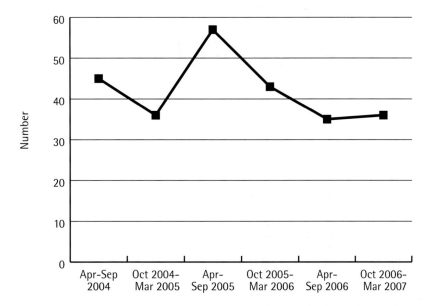

The most notable reduction was in criminal damage, which showed a year-on-year decrease of 52% and a decline of 42% (Figure 16). However, the level of criminal damage rose again in the period after the end of the order, by 36%, but remained lower than the level at the same time the previous year (a decline of 21%).

Figure 16: Types of crime in Northston

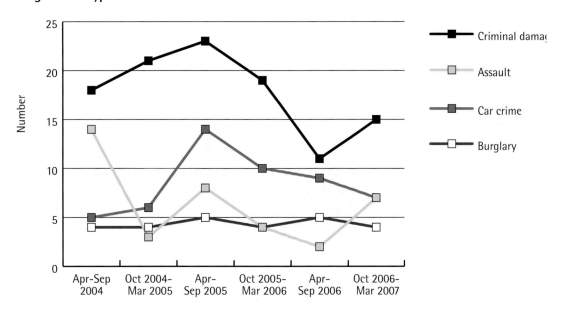

Figure 17 shows reports to the police of ASB incidents in Northston over the last three years.[19] The data show a significant increase in reported ASB in the first month of the dispersal order, which may have been a product of the initiative encouraging greater levels of reporting. Subsequently, there is a general downward trend, which resulted in the usual peak in August being avoided in 2007. This downward trend appears to have been sustained over the six months since the end of the dispersal order. Nevertheless, over the six months of the dispersal order the total number of ASB incident reports declined by 45% as compared to the same period in the previous year.

Figure 17: Reports of ASB in Northston (2004–07)

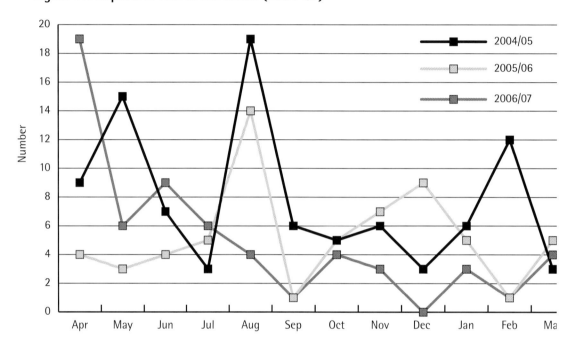

The neighbouring dispersal zone

The crime data for the neighbouring dispersal zone show a very slight increase (6%) in total crime during the order as compared to the previous year, but demonstrate a significant decrease (26%) on the previous six months (Figure 18). This decline has continued in the post-dispersal period.

Figure 18: Recorded crime in neighbouring dispersal zone

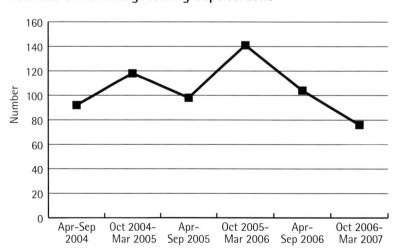

---

[19] The recording of ASB incidents changed over this period, usually in response to Home Office guidance.

An examination of the different types of crime reveals that changes in criminal damage underlie this trend (Figure 19). While the levels of criminal damage during the dispersal order period are very similar to those a year earlier, they represent a decrease on the previous six months (47%). This decline has been sustained over the post-implementation period.

Figure 19: Types of crime in neighbouring dispersal zone

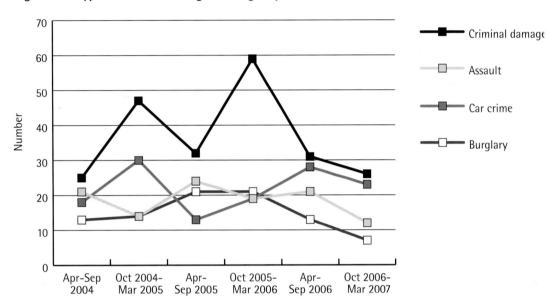

The dispersal order in the neighbouring area appears to have had less impact on reported incidents of ASB. The data show an 18% increase of reported ASB during the six months of the dispersal order as compared to the same period the previous year. However, they also indicate a significant 23% reduction in reported incidents as compared to the six months preceding the order. The data show a 40% reduction in the six months after the order as compared to the same period the previous year. If this is evidence of a post-dispersal order impact, it appears to have worn off as the last four months showed a steady increase.

Crime displacement

Prior to the implementation of both dispersal orders the police had identified two nearby areas judged the most likely to experience any displacement. Consequently, the police sought to counter this by dedicating additional patrols to these locations. Despite this, it appears that the dispersal orders displaced crime and ASB into one of the 'at risk' displacement areas.

During the dispersal order period crime rose by 148% on the previous six months and by 83% on the same period the previous year (Figure 20), against a background of an otherwise stable level of crime.

The data show the level of crime returning to previously normal levels in the six months after the end of the order. Displacement is most apparent for criminal damage, which rose by 388% on the previous six months and 290% year on year. Smaller increases are also detectable for burglary and car crime, of 100% and 67% respectively over the previous year's figures. While we need to be careful not to overinterpret these findings, there is evidence of a considerable displacement effect. As this neighbourhood is located between the two dispersal zones it may have experienced displacement arising from both locations. Evidence suggests that displacement from the neighbouring dispersal zone (rather than

Figure 20: Crime in identified displacement area

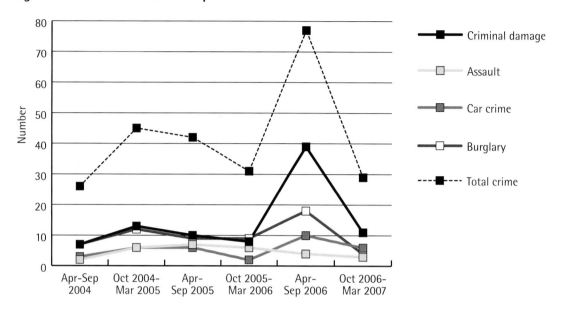

Northston) was more prevalent. These data support information provided by young people and local residents in interviews regarding the movement of disorder. A local police officer commented:

'What we found is that the congregation of groups, anti-social behaviour and other related crimes are happening in these displacement zones. So that's a negative side of things. Some will go home but some will go to these displacement areas.' (Middle-ranking police officer)

These concerns were reinforced by the apparent displacement effect revealed in the reported ASB data (Figure 21). During the six months of the Northston dispersal order reported incidents of ASB in the neighbouring displacement area increased by 20%, as

Figure 21: Reports of ASB in identified displacement area (2004-07)

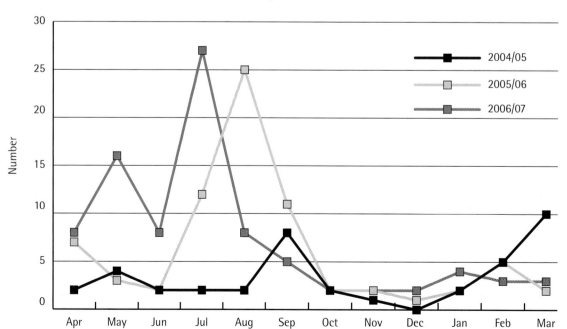

compared to the same period in the previous year. Evidence from young people and the police suggests additional displacement of ASB to residential areas further afield.

Nonetheless, a similar pattern of crime displacement was not evidenced in a second pre-identified displacement area, situated adjacent to Northston's neighbouring dispersal zone.

Southby

The research compared levels of crime and ASB reports to the police within the confines of the dispersal zone, the local ward and the wider borough. The crime and ASB reports data were collected for three periods of time: (i) the period of the dispersal order; (ii) the six months immediately preceding the introduction of the order; and (iii) the six-month period that corresponded to the dispersal order from the previous year to enable year-on-year comparisons. As the order terminated on 31 January 2007 it was not possible within the fieldwork period to collect data on the six months after the order ended.

Figure 22 shows that recorded crime in Southby decreased during the period of the dispersal order as compared to the preceding six months (by 15.3% in the dispersal zone and 3% across the ward as a whole), but increased as compared to the same period the previous year (by 9.3% in the dispersal zone and 11.1% across the entire ward). By contrast, crime across the borough increased during this period by 10.6% as compared to the same period a year earlier and by 3.4% as compared to the six months preceding the order. These figures suggest that the reduction in recorded crime on the previous six months and the slow-down in the year-on-year increase might reflect a positive impact of

Figure 22: Recorded crime, Southby

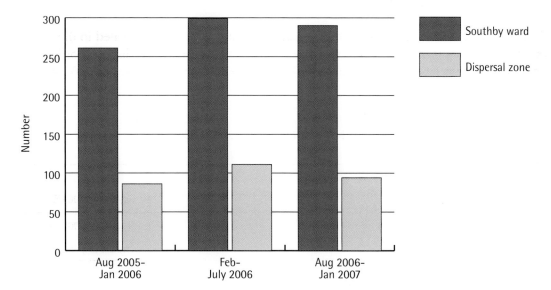

the dispersal order. A closer analysis of the types of crime where reductions were most prominent indicates otherwise. Offences of criminal damage and shoplifting increased both on the previous six-month period and the same period the previous year.

During the dispersal order, calls to the police increased significantly, as compared both with the previous six months and the same six months the previous year.[20] Borough wide, calls to the police increased by 113% on the same period in 2005/06 and by 127%

---

[20] Changes to the classification system for incoming calls to the police, undertaken part way through the dispersal order, are likely to have skewed these data by adding to the upward trend.

on the previous six months. Increases in Southby, however, were greater. Calls in the dispersal zone increased by 312% on the same period the previous year and by 390% on the six months preceding the dispersal order. The figures for the ward showed an increase of 285% and 276% respectively (Figure 23). Taking into consideration changes in classification, calls to the police increased during the implementation of the dispersal order. Where the data are available, they show that over three quarters of all calls from the dispersal zone concerned rowdy or inconsiderate behaviour and street drinking.

Figure 23: Number of calls to the police, Southby

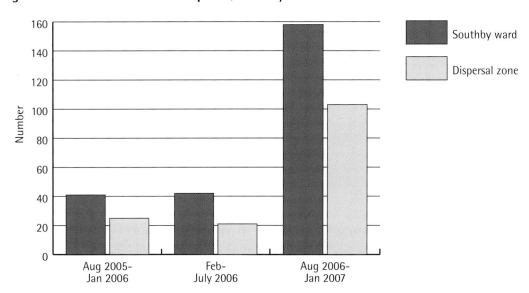

The interview and survey data report considerable evidence of displacement to neighbouring streets just outside the dispersal zone. People were concerned that while the area around the shops had become safer during the dispersal order period, the back streets and some of the green spaces had become less safe:

> 'The groups of young people who were dispersed simply moved to an area just beyond the boundaries of the order and regrouped.' (Resident)

A young person highlighted a 'ping-pong'-like effect of dispersal orders:

> 'If you've got a dispersal order in [this area] then everyone goes to [the neighbouring area]. You put it in there, they're all going to come back again, aren't they?'

At a wider level, displacement encouraged a 'domino' effect, whereby an order in one area had helped to provoke dispersal orders in neighbouring areas. There was evidence that this occurred in the north of the borough where dispersal order use had been considerably higher than the south. This phenomenon is not explained by higher levels of ASB. The significant mobility of young people facilitated by free bus travel and discounted underground fares made displacement a considerable issue. A police officer noted with some irony: 'The Oyster card has made life easier for them [young people] and a bit more tricky for us to police'. A semi-official policy of staggering the introduction of dispersal orders in neighbouring areas has been one way of 'keeping youths on the move'.

Some youths who said that they had been dispersed described the game-like quality of 'cat and mouse' interactions with the police promoted by the dispersal order. They claimed to derive 'fun' out of provoking the police to chase them, then splitting up only to congregate again later. Thus, flouting authority became a routine pastime.

Young people and adult residents' surveys

Young people attending two schools just outside the boundaries of the dispersal zones were asked whether they felt safer in groups or alone when they went out in public (Figure 24). Across both schools, more than half (52%) said they felt safest in large groups (of six or more) and a further 30% in smaller groups. By contrast, only 11% replied that they felt most safe out with one other person and 7% said they felt safest by themselves. Generally, girls were more likely to prefer large groups and boys were more likely to reply that they felt safest by themselves. Those aged 16 or over were more likely to feel safe out by themselves and those aged 13 to 15 were more likely to feel safe in groups.

Figure 24: Young people's perceptions of safety (%)

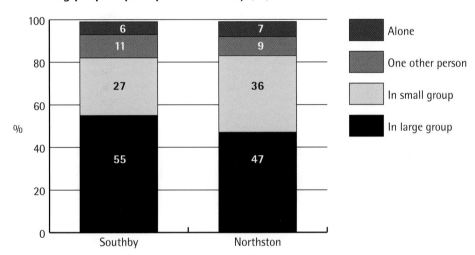

For many young people, gathering in groups presented a paradox in that they derived feelings of greater safety from being in a group, but also experienced encountering large groups as potentially threatening. They were aware that in groups they might appear intimidating to others. In focus group interviews two young males tried to explain the ambiguous relationship between risk, safety and being in groups:

'You feel more safe when you're with more people, but other people don't feel safe when you're with more people ... do you know what I mean?'

'If you're with a gang, you look intimidating but it's safer ... safety in numbers.'

Many were concerned with the manner in which all young people gathering in groups were perceived as problematic. A 13-year-old girl commented:

'I can see why people see a big group as a problem, and some big groups are a problem, but then they think that every single big group is a problem. You could have a few people causing trouble and then the majority of people think that every young person hanging out in a group is going to try and cause trouble.'

Young people generally reported higher levels of having been a victim of ASB in the area immediately around the dispersal zone in the previous 12 months than adults (Table 5). Younger residents, notably those under the age of 30, were more likely to report significantly higher levels of victimisation than older residents.

Table 5: Victim of ASB in the previous 12 months (%)

	Northston	Southby
Young people survey	38	40
Residents' survey	34	30

The majority of young people attending the schools did not live in the locality. This partly explains the relatively lower number of young people who were aware of the existence of the dispersal order, notably in Southby (Table 6). Nevertheless, the young people represented were those who visited the dispersal order areas at least sometimes. The comparative data suggest that the communication strategy in Southby was less effective than in Northston. Undoubtedly, the geographic layout of Northston combined with the greater investment in publicising the order through local newsletters and school visits, helped spread awareness of the dispersal order.

Table 6: Knowledge of the dispersal order (%)

	Northston	Southby
Young people survey	62	16
Residents' survey	85	54

Over a third of young people in Southby (37%) and nearly a half in Northston said that the reasons for the order had not been explained to them. By contrast, 56% of residents in Southby and 68% in Northston said that the reasons had been adequately explained to them.

Most residents said that they felt confident that they understood, at least partly, the dispersal powers that were available to the police as well as the boundaries of the designated area (Figures 25 and 26), albeit there was greater confidence about the former

Figure 25: Levels of understanding about the dispersal powers (%)[a]

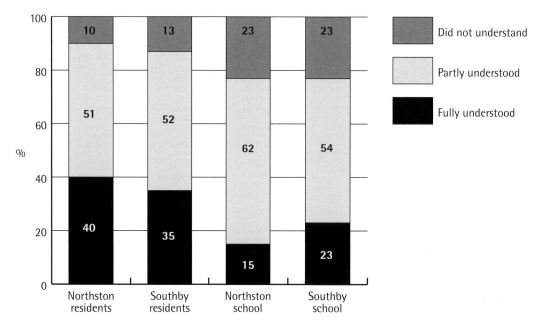

Note: [a]Figures may add up to more than 100% due to rounding.

Figure 26: Levels of understanding about the dispersal order boundaries (%)

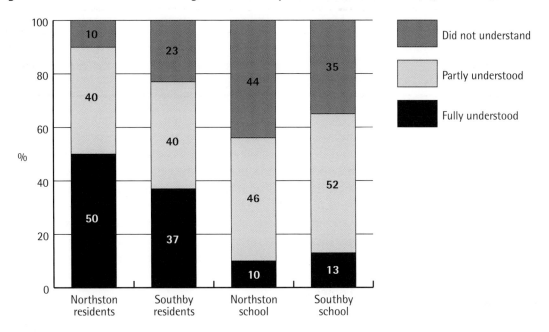

than the latter. Approximately a quarter of young people in both sites said they did not understand the powers and nearly two fifths said that they did not understand the boundaries of the zones. This was particularly marked among the Northston school pupils. Collectively, the data show a sizeable minority of residents and young people with whom communication appears not to have been effective in outlining the parameters of the dispersal order and the powers to which it gave rise.

The youth focus groups exposed uncertainty and confusion about dispersal orders. Young people and adults frequently described the dispersal powers as a 'curfew order', despite the fact that the escort powers were not implemented in one of the sites for most of the duration of the order (given the then legal uncertainties).

There was evidence from residents in both case study sites of a strongly held 'narrative of decline'; in which social relations were perceived to be deteriorating. Disorder and ASB from youths were often highlighted as indicators of this decline. This narrative was particularly marked in Northston. Similar surveys carried out in 2001 allowed us to chart this decline in perceptions about the community (Figure 27). There were recorded declines

Figure 27: Changing perceptions of Northston residents (2001/07) (%)

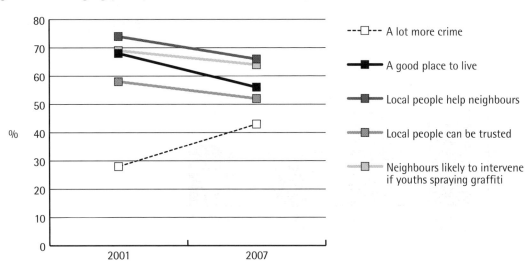

in perceptions about the extent to which local people: are believed to help neighbours; consider the area to constitute a close-knit community; think local people can be trusted; feel that people get along with each other; and share similar values.

Two thirds of residents in both areas thought that ASB had increased in the previous two years. In Northston, two thirds of residents thought that crime had increased over the same period, compared to slightly over half of residents in Southby. In both areas this is much higher than the national average, recorded by the British Crime Survey, which found that 42% of people thought that crime was increasing in their local area; 15% 'a lot more' and 27% 'a little more' (Nicholas et al, 2007). That few respondents discriminated between ASB and crime reflects the uncertainties people harbour about the relationship between the two and the manner in which they are often confused in public debate and practice.

When asked whether the area had become more or less safe as a result of the introduction of the dispersal order the most frequent response was that it had not changed (Table 7). Nevertheless, just over a third of residents in both areas said that the area was safer. Over a fifth of young people said that the area had become safer in Southby, albeit one in seven young people said that it had become less safe.

Table 7: Area has become safer/less safe as a result of the dispersal order (%)[a]

	Northston	Southby
Young people survey	22/6	22/14
Residents' survey	35/5	34/3

Note: [a]The data are based only on residents and young people who said that they knew about the dispersal order.

Across the two case studies, adult residents shared similar views about the impact of the dispersal order (Figure 28). At least half agreed that there were not enough places for young people to go (72% in Southby and 58% in Northston) and that the order provided a short-term response that did little to address longer-term issues (63% in Northston and 49% in Southby). While only a small number of residents felt that the order unfairly targeted

Figure 28: Residents' views (% 'agreed')

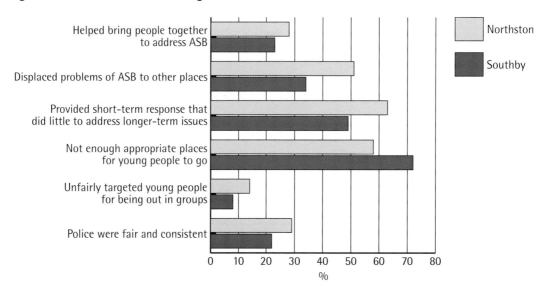

young people (14% in Northston and 8% in Southby), this figure was higher among parents with children over 10 years old.

Just under half (48%) of young people surveyed in Northston and 61% in Southby said that they were (at least slightly) more aware of the potential to cause anxiety to others as a result of the dispersal order and associated developments. Figure 29 shows that about half of pupils agreed that the order reminded them of the need to respect others in public (52% in Southby and 47% in Northston). In both areas a slightly smaller number of young people were as likely to disagree as to agree that the order had made the area a safer place for all ages.

Figure 29: Impact of dispersal order on young people (% 'agreed')

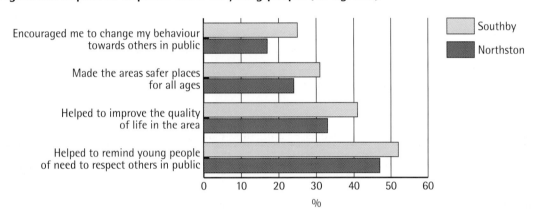

Nearly half of young people thought that they needed to take greater responsibility for the way their behaviour can intimidate others (Figure 30). The majority of young people in both areas said that there were not enough public places for young people to go – 56% in Northston and 57% in Southby. A significant number of young people agreed that the order had increased conflict between young and old people (46% and 39%).

Generally, young people in Southby were more critical of the dispersal order than in Northston where various attempts were made to engage with young people through the local schools. In Southby 61% agreed that the dispersal order was unfairly targeted at young people compared to 43% of youths in Northston. Nonetheless, 35% of youths in Southby agreed that the police were fair and consistent in their use of dispersal powers

Figure 30: Young people's views (% 'agreed')

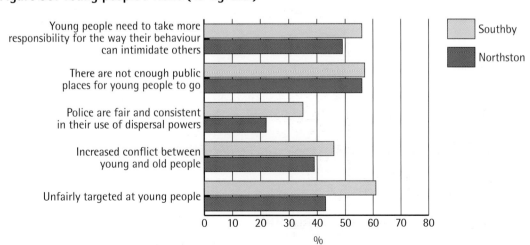

while 29% disagreed. This compares to 22% who agreed and 19% who disagreed in Northston.

By contrast, young people in Northston appeared to have a more negative view of the police as a result of the order (Figure 31). Nearly five times as many young people in Northston said that the policing of the dispersal order had left them feeling more negative towards the local police compared to those who said it had left them feeling more positive towards the police (51% and 11% respectively). Most of those who expressed negative feelings said that this was 'much more negative'. In Southby, by contrast, a greater proportion of young people said that the experience had left them feeling more positive (28%) than negative (16%).

Figure 31: Impact of dispersal order on youths' feelings towards local police (%)

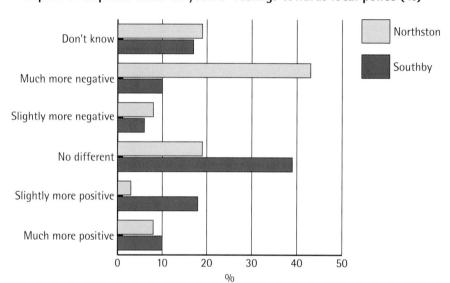

Young people dispersed

In Southby, 49 young people (nearly a fifth of all those who said they visited Southby at least sometimes) claimed to have been dispersed by the police and nearly one third knew someone who had been dispersed. In Northston, 30 young people said they had been dispersed by the police and one third knew someone who had been dispersed. Boys, unsurprisingly, were more likely to report having been dispersed. Those who said they had been dispersed were slightly older than the average respondent and their ethnic profile corresponded closely to the general profile of respondents. Of these, nearly half had been dispersed more than once and over a third (27%) three or more times. Figure 32 presents the aggregated responses from both areas outlining the impact on those who had been dispersed.

Young people reported mixed experiences of being dispersed. While 44% agreed that the police explained the reasons for exercising their powers, a similar number, 42%, disagreed. Half disagreed with the statement that the police listened to what they had to say. Just over a third (35%) felt that the police had treated them with respect, but a slightly larger number disagreed (37%). Two fifths (40%) said that the experience had left them with less confidence in the police, albeit over a quarter (29%) disagreed with this statement.

The focus groups with young people revealed much uncertainty about whether someone had formally been dispersed. They suggested that police regularly approached young

Figure 32: Impact of dispersal order on youths in Northston and Southby (*n*=79)

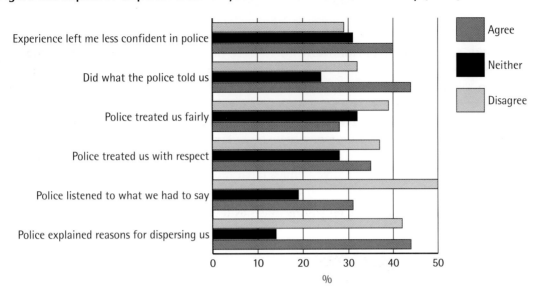

people to inform them to leave the area or that they should be going home due to the dispersal powers:

> 'Since the dispersal, lots of special police people have been going around and saying "it's getting late now, you should go home". They just said it's coming up to the dispersal time, you're going to have to split up or go home.'

Young people often differentiated between police who 'actually talk to you and listen to your point of view', as compared to those who did not listen to them.

Assessments by professionals

A police officer described the dispersal order as having three wider functions or by-products: first, as 'a way of getting a community to come to life' by creating a brief respite, focusing attention and galvanising coordinated activity; second, as 'a conversational tool' to focus dialogue; and third, as a means 'to lever additional funding into an area', particularly with regard to youth provision and diversionary activities, as well as additional police cover in the short term.

Some professionals in both areas felt that more might have been done to ensure a long-term legacy by ensuring that all partners were 'on board' before the start of the order, rather than trying to use the order as a way of formulating a partnership approach:

> 'What needs to happen is a more coordinated approach to resolving the issues in the longer term. Because running alongside a dispersal zone, if we'd had in place some efforts to say "We don't want you hanging about on the green because there's damage, there's beer cans, there's litter, there's all sorts of problems. But this is what we're offering as a replacement", then that would have worked particularly well because you could have given them the alternative rather than just saying; "right, disappear".' (Middle-ranking police officer)

Similarly, in both areas there were concerns expressed by some that implementing an order before having the necessary diversionary activities in place was tantamount to 'putting the cart before the horse':

'My personal opinion is we went too quickly, going for the dispersal zone. I don't think we've looked at diversion first.... Youth services knew nothing about it, until I joined them in the loop. That to me says we're not doing the problem-solving properly. We are just doing enforcement.' (Middle-ranking police officer)

The focused attention provided by a dispersal order was seen to constitute a vital opportunity that needed to be exploited to its fullest. While there was an attempt in Northston by the police to engage the local schools, including 'citizenship' presentations, in both areas it was felt that more might have been done in partnership with the schools.

In Southby, the absence of alternative venues led a mother of one teenager resident in the area to take it upon herself to open up her garage to her son and friends so that they could congregate and listen to music. While this was identified as a success by the police, in that it reflected a willingness on the part of the community to take responsibility for local problems, it also highlighted the inadequacies of local youth facilities. Crucially, this meant local authorities and other service providers playing a central role in facilitating preventive and diversionary activities:

'I am not sure that as a police service we are ever going to stop kids hanging around on the street corners, until and unless the local authorities are in a position to supply proper diversionary activities. I think that would require a significant culture change.' (Police manager)

In Northston, one enduring legacy was the decision taken shortly after the end of the designation period to reopen the library as a youth centre, in the light of the decision to relocate the library within the community to the primary school. Youth services were exploring with young people proposals regarding the nature of the facilities. However, there was some debate as to whether the dispersal order itself had had any direct relationship to this commitment to youth provision. For many, the most salient benefits of the order derived from its capacity to generate a dialogue with all relevant sections of the community:

'I would argue that just having the ability, or the opportunity for us to engage with kids, has got to be good. The vast majority of kids I think will understand that if they cross that boundary of being anti-social, they will expect something to happen. I see our responsibility as actually informing them, educating them, advising them in that respect. To get that dialogue, I think, is useful. Because as a kid I wouldn't have known what is anti-social and what is not. It's subjective, isn't it?' (Police manager)

In Northston, the dispersal orders unintentionally provoked a wider discussion about the limits of such an approach. A youth worker involved in the local community explained:

'When the dispersal order finally came around, I thought well actually, ironically it might well be an interesting stimulus for discussion.... More recently I've been in meetings where people are starting to say "well, there are limits to enforcement". And in one of the last meetings I went to, people were saying "maybe we need to start looking at the roots of this".'

Project workers were able to use the controversy and interest generated by the exceptional nature of the dispersal orders to focus attention on their intergenerational project. While working directly with a relatively few residents, there was some evidence from the residents' survey that the project encouraged a more informed dialogue about behaviour, local perceptions and tolerance. The same youth worker explained the role the dispersal order played in this wider work:

'What's been a fascination to me is what the dispersal order did in terms of catalysing other things.... And indeed in terms of facilitating debate. And some of the work that's gone on, in terms of facilitating a dialogue between young people and the police, it's been pretty good.... If you get issues in communities – the dispersal order and the need for it being one of them – then the resolution of these problems comes at least in part from a better conversation going on between the protagonists.'

As well as providing a respite, dispersal orders due to their exceptional nature and powers serve as a wake-up call to prompt action. The rigours that attend to authorisation and the publicity that designation demands send out a clear message to local people and relevant agencies that something needs to be done to address local problems through collective action. It acts as a focal point to galvanise strategic thinking and coordinated activity:

'The dispersal zone has brought a lot of media attention, local resident attention and police attention to [ASB in the community]. And the issues have become much more apparent and therefore there are a lot more resources and effort going into it. So they've worked hand in hand particularly well. Because a lot of what we are doing in the dispersal zone would have happened anyway with the advent of neighbourhood policing but I suppose what a dispersal zone does is it clarifies what your issues and your objectives are.' (Middle-ranking police officer)

Others were more circumspect about the quality of the dialogue and engagement that the order generated:

'It doesn't actually resolve anything. At the beginning of the process we had a situation whereby we'd got young people that were disengaged from the adult community. We'd got adults that were disengaged from the young people's community. Six months later we've still got that situation. We've still got groups of young people that won't engage with adults and vice versa. Very little has happened as a direct result of the dispersal order in terms of addressing those two separate poles.' (Housing officer)

On reflection, many professionals felt that although a certain amount of headway had been made during the order there was a danger that the 'head of steam' generated might dissipate in much the same way that the orders in both areas were allowed to 'peter out'.

6
Policing and young people

David Blunkett, reflecting on the development of dispersal powers, commented:

'People said they wouldn't work but actually they have. The downside of them is we didn't build in the corollary which was that if we're going to deal with youngsters over a three-month or six-month period, then you have to do something pretty profound while you've got that opportunity. While you've clamped down and restored some sort of order, it needs to be an opportunity to put longer-term solutions in place rather than just see it as an oppressive measure. Although in some areas the curfew has been used as a very positive way of achieving that, it hasn't universally been the case.' (Personal interview, January 2007)

The short-term nature of the dispersal order is both a strength and weakness. Its strength lies in the window of opportunity it provides for more fundamental thinking, planning and dialogue. As an exceptional measure it can provoke action and stimulate genuinely joined-up problem-solving endeavours. Its weakness lies in the fact that in itself it is not a solution to problems of disorder and insecurity and cannot be presented as such without fuelling inappropriate public expectations.

Our research suggests that dispersal orders can be effective in drawing additional police resources into a dedicated area and galvanising local attention to the problem of ASB and perceptions of insecurity. As visible policing is a limited public resource with significant competing demands, dispersal orders can become seen as a way of attracting or capturing, at least for a short time, more police patrols. Local residents' groups and politicians were well aware of this:

'There's a clear instruction [to the police to] walk around the dispersal zones, so much so that the neighbouring areas are saying "we're not seeing them". And the next thing I can see happening is the neighbouring areas will be saying well we want one too. And if you're not very careful you've got an exponential growth here which outstrips supply.' (Councillor, Yorkshire)

The geographical and social map of dispersal order use does not correspond straightforwardly to the distribution of risks of victimisation. This raises concerns over the extent to which certain communities and businesses are able to use their capacity to articulate concerns about ASB to influence dispersal order authorisation, primarily as a means of drawing police resources into an area. The national establishment of local procedures to respond to 'community call for action' (required under the 2004 Police and Justice Act) may further encourage this possibility by instituting additional channels of complaint.

Discretionary policing and summary powers

There has been a significant and marked drift towards policing through 'summary justice' in recent years. This has been most evident in the expansion, and expanded enforcement, of fixed penalty notices particularly with regard to disorder. The fact that police CSOs, as well as local authority officers and 'accredited persons', can enforce penalty notices for disorder (PNDs) has also served to increase their use.[21] In 2006/07, the number of PNDs issued across England and Wales rose to approximately 125,000, constituting some 9% of all detections (Nicholas et al, 2007). Allied to this has been the introduction of highly discretionary police powers and an increase in the powers of police officers to impose directions with breach being a criminal offence.

Dispersal orders are a notable example of this trend. Often new powers have been introduced initially as exceptional powers, by way of being time limited or area based, only for them later to become normal aspects of policing. This normalisation of exceptional powers is evidenced in the introduction of designated public places orders (under the 2001 Criminal Justice and Police Act, s.13), which provide police and CSOs with powers to require people to stop drinking or to confiscate alcohol within controlled drinking zones in areas that have experienced alcohol-related disorder or nuisance. More recently, police powers have been extended to allow officers to give direction to leave a locality (for up to 48 hours) to someone who is likely to cause or to contribute to the occurrence of alcohol-related crime or disorder in that locality (2006 Violent Crime Reduction Act, s. 27). This new power comes with no prior need for designation. There are direct analogies here with the recent proposals to normalise dispersal powers by allowing police to disperse individuals without the need for any prior designation of a given area (Home Office 2006b).

As the quotation from David Blunkett reported in Chapter 2 highlights, the current vogue for giving the police wider discretionary powers to tackle ASB risks ignoring the fundamental lessons of history and taking us back to pre-1984 'sus' laws with all the negative implications for police–community relations.

Policing and procedural justice

As they provide police with powers to enforce non-compliance with police directions, dispersal orders can become bound up with judgements about the manner in which (young) people respond to officers' decisions or question their authority. In such circumstances, perceptions of those dispersed regarding the legitimate authority of the officer will be shaped by the apparent fairness of the direction, the appropriate manner in which the police exercise their powers, explain their reasoning, listen to what those subject to the direction have to say and treat them with respect. In short, compliance will be strongly influenced by perceptions of procedural fairness. A youth articulated how a reasoned explanation can have implications for compliance:

> 'You don't feel so hard done by when [the police] explain why they have got to do it, why they have got to split you up. If they just say: "right, you have all got to go back to where you come from", you feel a bit hard done by because you think "oh, we haven't done anything wrong, why should we go back because some

---

[21] PNDs, originally introduced by the 2001 Criminal Justice and Police Act, are now available for 16- and 17-year-olds. Schemes for their use in relation to 10- to 16-year-olds have been piloted in seven police force areas, with a view to extension across the country.

police officer decided that we had to?" But then, if they explain why they have got to split you up it is different.' (15-year-old male)

Another youth who had been dispersed made a related observation:

'As long as [the police] said "just keep your noise down" and stuff like that and "you can stay as long as you keep your noise down", we'd say "okay that's fair, that's fair" and you agree with them. But otherwise you start giving them lip.'

As this implies, perceptions of unfairness may not only have negative implications for compliance but also provoke active defiance. There is now a substantial body of research demonstrating that experiences of procedural justice can significantly affect perceptions of legitimacy and public confidence in the police as well as legal compliance (Sunshine and Tyler, 2003). A major review of policing research has noted:

Modest but consistent scientific evidence supports the hypothesis that the less respectful police are towards suspects and citizens generally, the less people will comply with the law. Changing police 'style' may thus be as important as focusing police 'substance'. Making both the style and substance of police practices more 'legitimate' in the eyes of the public, particularly high-risk juveniles, may be one of the most effective long-term police strategies for crime prevention. (Sherman et al, 1997, Chapter 8: pp 1-2)

The greater emphasis within summary policing on matters of 'substance' at the expense of 'style' may undermine police legitimacy and hence effectiveness. That many of the young people who said they had been dispersed reported feeling unfairly treated is worrying, as is the more general finding that young people said their feelings towards the local police had deteriorated due to the dispersal order.

Recent research shows that the impact on perceptions towards the police of having a bad experience during an encounter with the police is four to 14 times as great as that of having a positive experience (Skogan, 2006). Being treated unfairly plays a significant factor in this. Furthermore, the negative consequence of perceptions of unfair treatment attain not only to the individuals directly concerned but can have vicarious implications for others as encounters are recounted to a wider network of friends who may share in the perceived indignity. A youth explained:

'If you hear one of your friends getting dispersed, you get angry. You want to stick up for your friend. So, the next time [the police] come up to you, you're more reluctant to listen to the police.'

The discretionary nature and subjective interpretation of dispersal powers leave considerable scope for inconsistent implementation in ways that may impact negatively on perceptions of procedural fairness. Dispersing some young people and not others may be seen as arbitrary and procedurally unfair. Several police managers recognised the difficulties of ensuring consistent enforcement practices in dispersal zones. Police recognised that internal communication among police and partner organisations is as important as external communication to the public or through the press.

'That's been a particular frustration, even amongst cops as well, misunderstandings, inappropriate use of terminology by our staff, people calling it an exclusion order or a curfew zone, all this type of thing.' (Middle-ranking police officer)

Young people in the case study sites clearly differentiated between local police officers who they were more likely to know by sight and who were more likely to know something about the locality and other officers who they believed lacked the same understanding of the area and its people:

> 'The ones who don't know who you are and what you have been doing, they stick right by the rule book, but the ones that you do know, they reason with you, "stay out of trouble", "don't start getting rowdy" and they give you a chance.' (15-year-old male)

If the ultimate aim is to foster among young people an understanding of the inappropriateness of certain behaviours in public places, then experiences of procedural justice in the use of discretionary police powers are vital. If summary justice through policing is experienced as arbitrary or discriminatory it is likely to have little or no positive impact on changing behaviour or influencing the values that young people hold regarding how their actions impact on others. Compliance in such a context, at best, will mean doing what they were already doing somewhere else outside the dispersal zone. At worse, such experiences and interactions may encourage a sense of injustice, which fuels defiance and amplifies deviant activity.

Relations between police and young people

Evidence from recent studies suggests that between a third and one half of all young people aged 11 to 15 have had experience of adversarial contact with the police (Anderson et al, 1994; Jamieson et al, 1999). Whereas most youths only have one contact with the police, increasing the level of contact can propel young people towards more enduring 'criminal careers'. While youth is a period of heightened offending, most juvenile offences are fairly minor and young people mostly desist from such group-related activities as they grow older. Young people's peak offending age lies between 14 and 18, after which time for most the prevalence of offending diminishes, regardless of interventions. Formal contact with the criminal justice system, however, tends to reduce the likelihood of desistance (Sherman et al, 1997). In a study of randomly assigned young offenders, Klein (1986) found that the more legalistic processing of a juvenile suspect, the higher the official recidivism rate. The underlying message from this body of research is that *minimal police and criminal justice intervention for many youths maximises their desistence from offending*.

This is not to suggest that for some young people early interventions are both unnecessary and ineffective. However, blanket powers that fail to discriminate between those engaged in significant and persistent criminal activities and those who are not, risk drawing youths into adversarial relations with the police. The group focus of dispersal powers is likely to constitute the means by which some young people first enter police records on the basis of who they associate with. Research suggests that youths often first come to the attention of the police as a result of the ('wrong') company they keep (McAra and McVie, 2005). Dispersal orders may exacerbate this effect by drawing to the attention of the police those who might otherwise not have been.

Given the importance of 'visible presence' within the application of the powers, police suspicion may rest on prior contact and acquaintance, appearance of social status and dress. Items of clothing worn by youths (such as baseball caps and hooded jackets) can render an individual suspicious in the eyes of the police (Quinton et al, 2000) and threatening to some members of the community. Young people in this research perceived this to be the case, with implications for their views on the efficacy and legitimacy of police practices. Furthermore, groups of young people in some dispersal zones are being targeted as much because their appearance, deportment or dress is perceived by others as 'intimidating' or 'unsightly', as for specific acts of ASB.

A 15-year-old highlighted the ambiguous impact of the dispersal order for many young people:

> 'They are good … I mean it stops other people feeling intimidated by bigger groups but sometimes it can be a bad thing because other friends who don't actually do things wrong get moved on because people take one look at them and assume they're doing something wrong. So, there's two sides of the story.'

The existence of dispersal powers can escalate intervention and increase police–youth antagonism. In one way, dispersal orders escalated intervention by generating information on young people who the police spoke to, warned or dispersed. These data were often used to precipitate other ASB-related interventions, from home visits and formal warnings to acceptable behaviour contracts. In another way, police often judged young people on the manner in which they reacted to warnings or directions to disperse:

> 'As soon as the police become involved, it's not just low-level anti-social behaviour any more because there's authority there in terms of the police. And you find [youths] react in one of two ways, they'll go somewhere else and carry on, or they'll take heed and go home and that's what it's all about … because a lot of the time you can tell them to go home or disperse, and a lot of the kids who are responsible go home.' (Middle-ranking officer, North Yorkshire Police)

The implications of this observation are twofold: first, directions to disperse are likely to have the greatest impact on those youths who are not genuinely 'anti-social', by curtailing the liberties of responsible young people who go home. Second, how someone responds to authority, whether with deference or defiance, becomes a, if not *the*, salient factor in subsequent authoritative assessments and decisions, more important potentially than the initial behaviour itself. The offence potentially committed, after all, is failure to comply with an officer's directions and does not necessarily relate to the seriousness of the original behaviour. Challenges to authority may lead to conflictual relations with the police more fundamentally than the behaviour that triggered the encounter. Young people were aware of this effect:

> 'If they didn't have a dispersal order, we wouldn't look as rebellious because we are just sat chilling, but if they split us up then we meet up again, so it makes us look like we are troublemakers.' (15-year-old male)

Our research suggests that increased levels of police contact may foster negative feelings towards the police, which in turn may amplify deviance. Where young people are indiscriminately labelled as problematic, to such a degree that their presence in public space is no longer tolerated, significant implications may arise for their collective and self-identity and the formation of youth subcultures:

> 'It has made us get into trouble with the police a lot more as we get into trouble for being in a certain area or being in a group of five or more…. Young people are behaving worse than before because they cannot hang around their own village.' (15-year-old female)

Alienating groups of young people who routinely spend time in public spaces may also reduce the flow of information to the police. Not only is 'community intelligence' vital for effective policing but young people are particularly likely to posses it, given the high level of youth victimisation and young people's frequent presence in public places. A police manager recognised the importance of not alienating youths:

'They're our main victim group and they're our main suspect group. So we should be engaging with those kids, whether they're standing on the street corner or not.' (Manager, Metropolitan Police)

The lesson from the early 1980s was that aggressive styles of policing could produce a vicious circle, whereby information from communities to the police dried up, rendering the police less effective and prompting increasingly intensive and discretionary forms of policing (Kinsey et al, 1985).

Young people who frequent public spaces and engage in 'street life' constitute 'easy pickings' for police attention, notably under pressures of meeting targets for the number of 'offences brought to justice'. Dispersal orders, by focusing police attention on what the ex-chair of the Youth Justice Board described as 'low hanging fruit' (Morgan, 2007), may serve to stigmatise and label groups of youths. While our research does not suggest that dispersal powers per se are directly criminalising large numbers of young people, due to the low rate and absolute numbers of arrests and offences they provoke, nevertheless they are widening the net of criminal justice intervention by lowering the threshold at which some young people come to the attention of the police. Against a background of decreasing aggregate crime, the 26% increase in the number of children and young people criminalised in the period 2002-06 is a worrying indication that, as a society, we may be unwittingly alienating a generation of young people with potentially significant long-term implications.

Communicative properties

Dispersal orders send out important symbolic messages and communicate values. Not only are media publicity and public communication central elements in implementing dispersal orders, but also the designation of exceptional powers to a specific locality emits messages about a place, its social relations, dominant values of order and general well-being. It seeks to convey signals about the types of behaviour that will and will not be tolerated, as well as appropriate responses to local complaints. For example, local councillors, and some police, viewed the authorisation of a dispersal order as sending a clear message to residents (and thus the local electorate) that they were 'doing something' tangible in response to concerns over safety and perceptions of insecurity. It constituted a high-profile response that was seen to speak directly to the often-heard grievance that 'nobody takes our complaints seriously'. In this sense, dispersal orders can have a decidedly political appeal. Not only do they communicate a willingness of authorities to act decisively but also that problems have deteriorated to such a state as to require drastic and exceptional action. Consequently, it could prompt others to seize the opportunity to make a difference. Some residents felt that the dispersal order, by indicating that authorities were being responsive to their concerns, was able to galvanise the local community, providing it with an opportunity to demonstrate that residents too could make a difference to the quality of life in their neighbourhood:

'I think that a number of local people who had felt intimidated and who didn't have any confidence in a police response, realised that they did have the ability to "do" something. Although I have intervened on a number of occasions when I have seen petty crime or vandalism committed, I get utterly frustrated when others will not do the same and reply "what's the point? The police take no notice!" The dispersal order showed that the police did take notice and I hope it will encourage people to act more responsibly within the community.' (Resident)

Police managers were aware of the need to be seen to be responding to public demands and the manner in which a dispersal order presents a very tangible, albeit limited, response:

> 'The public are demanding some sort of police action, and a dispersal order gives my officers that ability to say "Look, we've done something for you. I don't know about the rest; can't fix that yet".' (Manager, Metropolitan Police)

Other residents were acutely concerned by the negative impact on the perception of the locality in the local press and media generated by the publicity associated with designation. Young people also felt that the existence of a dispersal order gave a place a bad reputation, even if this was unwarranted:

> 'It gives the place more of a reputation. If you think about [the community], you didn't think it would be that bad but when it got a dispersal order, it makes you think it is a really rough area.' (13-year-old female)

By drawing attention to a problem of ASB a high-profile dispersal order could actually reinforce perceptions of insecurity and discourage people from using public spaces. This could undermine efforts to encourage more people to use local public spaces and hence create a safer environment. Ultimately, it was often the confused messages that the dispersal order conveyed to different groups regarding its purpose, scope and limitations that created some of the most vexed problems, notably for police officers charged with implementation:

> 'One thing that I've found frustrating throughout is continually trying to describe to people what it actually is and what it isn't.... It's this thing that everybody clings to as a cover-all for everything. You're constantly fighting against it all the time to say to people "This is what it is, these are the things we can do, these are the things we can't do".' (Middle-ranking officer, North Yorkshire Police)

For some residents, that a dispersal order had been introduced was a reflection of the lack of adequate communication both within the community and between local service providers. One resident believed that it signalled a need:

> 'to find out what young people in [the community] are lacking; what would benefit their lives. We need to create a safe area for young people to be heard, feel valued and learn to understand what adults and older residents would like. We all need to communicate in a non-controlling and non-punishing way.'

Some other residents offered a less favourable interpretation of motivations, implying that 'doing something' might merely distract attention:

> '[The police and local authority] don't know what else to do, so doing this instead of looking to solve a problem properly made it look as if something was being done to help the village.'

Similarly, other residents recognised that the growing gulf between generations constitutes a central cause of tensions:

> 'The dispersal order has given the intolerant residents support while persecuting the youngsters. In turn, the only thing this can achieve is rebellion by the youngsters. Teaching the older people to be more tolerant and maybe even try to understand the youth is the only way forward. There are a lot of respectful youths in [the area] who are just not given a chance, which leads to them rebelling.'

Young people and public space

There is strong evidence to suggest that children and young people's use of public spaces has decreased significantly since the 1970s (Bradshaw and Mayhew, 2005). The decline in children 'playing out' and restrictions on young people's 'freedom to roam' are largely a product of preoccupations with safety on the part of parents and other adults. The fear of danger has encouraged adults to restrict the public places in which young people can play or meet and their mobility more generally. In a risk-adverse culture, health and safety concerns and fears of being sued have led many local authorities to remove playgrounds or to make them less attractive to children (Wheway, 2005). In 1971 some 80% of seven- to eight-year-olds were allowed to go to school without adult supervision, but by 1990 the figure had fallen to 9% (Hillman et al, 1991). Recent research for the Children's Society's Good Childhood Inquiry (GfK NOP, 2007) provides evidence that the current generation of parents is less likely to allow their children out unsupervised than their parents. This is coupled by a growing perception that parents who let their children play in the street are uncaring and irresponsible.

The use of dispersal powers exposes a significant tension within public policy between the commitments outlined in *Every Child Matters* (DfES, 2003) and the fulfillment of the ASB agenda. At one moment youth are *at risk* and need both protection and to be listened to, at the next instance youth are *the risk*; to be feared and dispersed. Both these sentiments were reflected in residents' views of young people. Dispersal orders conform with, and some might argue fuel, the latter sentiments. They convey stark negative messages to young people about their status in society and how they are perceived by adults.

For many young people the combination of the indiscriminate nature of the dispersal order and its focus on them seemed especially unfair. On one hand, they felt that insufficient differentiation is made between those young people simply hanging around in groups and those who actually engage in ASB; on the other, they remarked on the failure to target adults engaged in ASB. Adult residents also expressed that they were concerned about the capacity of dispersal orders 'to tar all children and young people with the same brush':

> 'I believe that the dispersal order has given young people feelings of unfairness and injustice. It just gives them a reason to be angry. Teenagers need to be accepted and celebrated for their contribution to society, not shunned. But now older people see any gathering of young people as anti-social. In my understanding, the dispersal order has widened the misunderstanding between all.' (Resident)

A 15-year-old girl articulated more widely held concerns:

> 'Some of the powers, like being able to take us home after nine or disperse us, they make it out that we're all doing something wrong. It puts across the message that every young person is delinquent. We're always portrayed for the bad things that some of us do, it's never the good things.'

The introduction of the Mosquito device in one case study area clearly reinforced this message that all young people are problematic regardless of their actual behaviour. The device, which is now being installed in areas across the country, appears to afford a techological means of dispersing all youths from specific locations without any notion of what to say to them, how to engage them or how to socialise them. It lacks any attempt to inculcate pro-social behaviour or moral values, but instead emits a droning noise that implicitly says 'go away'.

Yet for many young people, meeting peers in local public spaces constitutes a fundamental aspect of developing their own sense of identity, and provides space in which to forge their independent capacity to manage risk and danger. In the absence of suitable alternative venues, public spaces constitute key resources for young people. Nevertheless, it is crucial that these spaces are safe for all to use without experiencing intimation or harassment.

Currently, under the remit of the 2003 ASB Act, youth are to be judged as much on the way they are perceived as by their actions. It is this that young people found so objectionable. They generally understood the need to act where genuinely ASB occurs, not least because they are most likely to be the victims of such behaviour. However, circumscribing their ability to congregate in public spaces in groups to them seemed unfair and unwarranted.

Some people felt that one question to which few were able to provide an adequate answer was: *where should dispersed youths go?* In the absence of a suitable answer some people feared that young people might either congregate in areas where they are more vulnerable or displace problems to other, potentially more vulnerable, communities. Dispersal orders are often situated in symbolic public spaces with local amenities that serve as meeting points and junctions for significant flows of pedestrians. Such locations tend to provide forms of natural surveillance, street lighting and the presence of 'capable guardians' conducive to rendering them relatively safe for young people. If policies are to be informed by concerns about the protection of young people then they might be better suited to fostering public spaces in which youth are encouraged to assemble for their own safety where there is a certain degree of adult oversight, not banished from central public spaces to lurk in the shadows:

> 'We have got nowhere to go anyway. We have got a youth club but it is only open three days a week.... So where else are we going to go, apart from the park? If we go to the park we get in trouble, so we can't do anything right.' (14-year-old male)

Some youths expressed concern that the dispersal order might be interfering with young people's ability to access important local resources, notably shops. A 15-year-old female commented that 'People feel that there is no freedom for them'. Some residents were sympathetic to the situation for young people:

> 'Positive steps have been, and are currently being, taken to address the problem. Definitely more leisure provision and activities for young residents would be positive by offering alternatives to hanging around in groups. I have grown up in [the community] and fully understand why young people hang around in the street; there are very limited alternatives.'

> 'Give these kids somewhere to meet and have fun, like we all had the chance to do when we were teenagers'.

The lack of alternative youth activities with a limited degree of adult supervision was a common refrain from residents in both case studies:

> 'Provide more places for youngsters to use their free time. Instead of using "police state" tactics of imposing curfews on the under-16s, youngsters should be encouraged to be more active in sports and outdoor activities and provided with facilities in the local area. There seems to be a popular trend in the mainstream media to demonise *all* teenagers, whereas it is actually only a small percentage of troublemakers.'

'If a "stick" is introduced there should be a "carrot" and I have not seen any evidence of a carrot in this case.'

A second question that few considered in detail or debated at any length was: *what constitutes acceptable youth behaviour?* While many involved in implementation stressed that merely being in a group in a dispersal zone did not, of itself, constitute grounds for dispersal, there was great uncertainty as to what young people might be able to do before their presence or behaviour became sufficiently problematic in the eyes of others:

'I don't remember being part of a discussion with anybody which talked about what the criteria for reasonable behaviour in [the community] is. I've got my own value judgements, but actually there isn't an agreement.' (Housing officer, Yorkshire)

This lack of clarity fuelled the concerns of young people over the uncertain and unpredictable response police officers might have to their presence in a dispersal zone. Many young people felt that dispersal powers provided too much scope for the police to base their judgements on stereotypes of appropriate or inappropriate clothing or demeanour.

Young people were keen to know precisely what they were allowed and not allowed to do in a dispersal zone. However, due to the subjective and context-specific nature of ASB as well as the compounding element of how their presence might be interpreted by others, this kind of prescriptive advice was rarely forthcoming. As a youth worker explained:

'What the young people also said they wanted was to posit certain scenarios: "If we were doing this would we get nicked?" That was a big thing for them. They didn't know, as nobody knows, which is part of the problem. You can't say you're going to get pulled for this, that and the other, because of the hugely significant point about interpretation.... And that's what confuses young people.... Of course, nobody can give them an answer and my experience is it depends on the old Bill that turn up!' (Youth worker, Yorkshire)

In a discussion about appropriate behaviour and respect a 13-year-old girl elaborated:

'If they [adults] had respect for us and didn't give us names and just think because we are a kid we are going to cause trouble, if they didn't do that then I think we would have a lot more respect for them, but as soon as they start looking at you as if you are rubbish and giving you a name, then obviously you aren't going to respect them.'

The theme of respect was important for most of the young people, albeit interpreted in a different way to that articulated within the Home Office Respect Agenda. In a focus group discussion about respect, two 15-year-old pupils commented:

'We have to respect the police, but I think the police should respect the younger people, they shouldn't just accuse you.' (female)

'You should be given the benefit of the doubt. Some people might be doing things they shouldn't but the majority won't. The police need to listen to young people more and understand that we don't go out to cause trouble.... If respect works both ways then people are more likely to respect the police even more.' (male)

Young people and risk

Negotiating risk is a prevalent aspect of how young people use public space. Youth surveys in the case study sites showed that over a third (37%) said that they had been the victim of ASB in the previous 12 months; nearly one fifth (19%) had been a victim either occasionally or regularly. The 2005 sweep of the Home Office survey of young people revealed that nationally over a quarter (27%) had been the victim of personal crime in the previous 12 months (Wilson et al, 2006: 67).[22] Those in the 10-15 age group were more likely to have been victims of personal crime than those aged 16-25.

Their frequent use of public space enables many young people to become highly aware of the topography of risks and dangers in their locality. As they derive feelings of safety from being in groups, there is considerable potential for dispersal to increase both young people's objective risks and subjective perceptions of risk. This was a recurring theme in the focus group interviews. Young people, notably girls, reported feeling safer in groups and therefore saw any attempt to disperse them as threatening their safety. One 13-year-old female raised the following rhetorical question: 'I think it's ridiculous because what if three people got split up and the one who goes on her own gets raped?'

All the police officers interviewed in the research insisted that under no circumstances would they ever require a group of young girls to disperse separately. Nevertheless, stories about this circulated among youths in both study areas. More significantly, the fact that this could be a possible interpretation of the powers highlighted ambiguities in the efficacy of dispersal. It reinforced a recurring theme that if young people are viewed as *a risk* to others, they are less likely to be seen as *at risk*.

This highlights a deep ambivalence regarding young people and public spaces within policy and media debates. On the one hand, children (and their parents) are told of the dangers to young people's health and well-being of sitting at home either in front of television sets or at internet-connected computer screens. On the other hand, when young people venture out in groups they are perceived as the source of danger. Evidence points to children and young people apparently becoming increasingly unhealthy, more prone to childhood obesity and less satisfied with their life and peer relations (UNICEF, 2007).

> 'We're already paying the price for effectively demonising and criminalising a generation.... Let's not beat about the bush, the anti-social behaviour agenda and respect agenda are not targeted at the wider community. They are targeted at particular minorities within it; young people.' (Youth worker, Yorkshire)

By telling young people in groups that they may be dispersed and/or escorted home because they are perceived to be intimidating to others, we may be in danger of reworking the traditional Victorian saying such that it now reads: *'Children should be not seen and not heard'*. Where taken too far, this may result in the erosion of the right to free assembly on the basis of uncertain or subjective judgements.

---

[22] The most common forms of victimisation were assault without injury (11%) and other personal thefts (9%).

Conclusions and policy implications

7

Dispersal orders, where well planned, can offer short-term respite to ASB and trigger longer-term problem-solving strategies in conjunction with key local partners. Symbolically, they can serve as a wake-up call to focus attention and galvanise energies to local troubles that have a significant impact on community well-being and the use of public spaces:

> 'I think it gave people breathing space and disrupted the habits of some young people, but it is only a sticking plaster.' (Resident)

> 'The reason why they're out on the streets is they've got to go somewhere, and kids will be kids. And I think that is the basic line. Kids will be kids, and they will be noisy, and they will show off, and they will damage things, because that's what they do. And what we're doing is just sticking plasters over this.' (Middle-ranking officer, Metropolitan Police)

A theme to emerge from this research is that the introduction of dispersal orders was prompted by, and justified in terms of, requests by the police for additional tools to assist them in managing ASB. Yet it is police officers who offer some of the most critical and reflective insights into the shortcomings of the powers and the challenges they entail. Through practice police have come to appreciate both the limitations and the unintended consequences of such sweeping and highly discretionary powers. There is a growing realisation among knowledgeable practitioners of the need to retain exceptional powers for focused, short-term and well-evidenced use.

Police officers felt that the powers to disperse were useful as tools of last resort, but many were also aware of the dangers to relations, with young people particularly, regarding overuse and inconsistent implementation. More often than not, the powers provided a framework for negotiation about the conditions of orderly behaviour. Police were also acutely aware of the dangers of falsely raising public expectations about the level of police patrols during the period of the dispersal order and the capacity of an enforcement strategy to solve problems of local disorder and insecurity.

Given the time-bounded nature of dispersal orders, managing an appropriate exit strategy and post-dispersal order policing plan presented significant challenges, notably as police often confronted calls for renewal. In an attempt to avoid publicity associated with the termination of an order, exit strategies were often unclear or deliberately downplayed as the policing initiative was allowed to dissipate quietly.

The window of opportunity created by dispersal order authorisation – where necessary, evidenced and proportionate – can be, and has been, used to effect change. Where this has happened it has combined a focus on prevention, problem-solving and diversionary activities for young people.

The benefits that stem from dispersal orders derive in large part from the process of authorisation and associated activities. They include:

- information-led policing through the analysis of ASB and crime-related trends;
- the community consultation, engagement and accountability engendered by the authorisation process;
- the increased level of visible policing necessitated to enforce the orders;
- the involvement of wider partner agencies in long-term strategic planning and problem-solving; and
- galvanising community capacity and dialogue about the appropriate use of public space, collective responsibility and tolerance.

These benefits do not necessitate the specific enforcement powers that dispersal orders facilitate. They might be achieved by other means. However, as associated with dispersal order designation they all derive from the fact that this is an exceptional response to specific problems in a manner that is both evidenced and considered proportionate. If the powers that currently accrue through dispersal designation were to become routine police powers (Home Office, 2007b), it is likely that the above benefits would be lost.

Where most effective, formal powers of dispersal are rarely deployed. Rather, policing tends to occur in the shadow of the powers; through the negotiation of order. In this, the powers become a vehicle for dialogue. This demands implementation by designated police knowledgeable about local people, places and problems. The blanket use of dispersal powers along the lines in which fixed notice penalties for disorder have been promoted would most likely be counterproductive for police–community relations.

Importantly, dispersal orders have significant communicative properties - the messages they send out to different groups – which are differently interpreted. As the research shows, these messages are often uncertain, mixed and imply different outcomes. Too often the meaning of an order is both confused and subject to misinterpretation. As such, dispersal orders provoke a 'communication battle' in which conveying appropriate messages becomes almost more important than the impact of policing and allied activities on the ground. In this, the media have a considerable role to play in the manner in which dispersal orders are interpreted and (mis)understood.

Dispersal order authorisation triggers exceptional powers, which are highly discretionary and summary in nature. Prior designation ensures that these powers are an appropriate, proportionate and planned response to repeated problems within a locality. Given the importance of prior designation and in accordance with best practice, *the authorisation process should be strengthened to require the police and local authority partners not only to state the grounds on which authorisation is sought but to provide appropriate evidence in support of such grounds.* A rigorous process of authorisation provides the subsequent designation, powers and associated initiatives with crucial procedural legitimacy and public accountability, and constitutes the reasoned basis on which local deliberations about long-term strategies can be founded.

As young people are most likely to be affected by dispersal powers given their use of public space, *specific consideration should be given in the authorisation process to consulting and engaging with young people who live in and use designated areas.*

The research revealed much confusion among the public and professionals about the purpose, nature and extent of dispersal powers. Most notable were uncertainties over whether the mere presence of groups in a designated area was sufficient to trigger the powers. Despite reassurances from police that the orders did not stop (young) people congregating, the fact that the law allows dispersal where the presence of groups 'has resulted, or is likely to result, in a member of the public being harassed, intimidated, alarmed or distressed' tended to undermine the veracity of such assurances. In this light, *consideration should be given to amending the existing law such that dispersal powers apply only to the **behaviour** of groups rather than merely their **presence***. This would align the law more closely with current police practice, remove considerable public confusion over the scope of the powers and reduce current perceptions that whole groups of young people are targeted by dispersal orders regardless of their actual behaviour.

In addition, there were considerable uncertainties about the value and effectiveness of the power to remove youths under 16 to their homes after 9pm from a designated zone. Many police forces preferred not to use this power.

Very little is known about the impact of dispersal orders on different groups in the population, notably in terms of ethnic origin. Given the discretionary nature of the powers, it is important that effective monitoring and evaluation are available to safeguard against unwarranted discrimination. As part of their duty under the 2000 Race Relations (Amendment) Act, the police and local authorities should ensure that they monitor the impact of dispersal powers on the promotion of race equality. *Government needs to secure rigorous monitoring systems and commission research to assess the impact and effectiveness of dispersal powers.*

The research reported here reinforces and reiterates the conclusions of the Public Accounts Committee (2007) report, among others, on the need for improved and standardised data collection systems that allow for better monitoring and evaluation of the effectiveness and impact of ASB powers. The report specifically called for greater knowledge about 'the extent to which socioeconomic, geographic, ethnic, and age factors influence the outcomes achieved' (House of Commons Committee of Public Accounts, 2007, p 5); a finding endorsed by this research.

Any proposed future dispersal powers that intend to circumvent the current authorisation process will remove a fundamental element of prior accountability and oversight of proportionality that exists within the current framework. Such proposals are likely to undermine police–community relations and exacerbate many of the policing challenges highlighted in this report. Furthermore, by normalising exceptional, time-limited powers any such proposals will erode the dispersal order's current role in triggering wider and longer-term problem-solving strategies. This research shows that where dispersal orders work best, their function as a catalyst for local dialogue and action that galvanises partnership activity is due in large part to their exceptional, time-bounded nature. Therefore, *no new powers should be introduced to give police officers on-the-spot dispersal powers without prior authorisation.*

References

Anderson, S., Kinsey, R., Loader, I. and Smith, C.G. (1994) *Cautionary Tales: Young People, Crime and Policing in Edinburgh*, Aldershot: Avebury.

Bradshaw, J. and Mayhew, E. (eds) (2005) *The well-being of children in the UK*, London: Save the Children.

Crawford, A., Lister, S. and Wall, D. (2003) *Great Expectations: Contracted Community Policing*, York: JRF.

Crawford, A., Lister, S., Blackburn, J. and Burnett, J. (2005) *Plural Policing: The Mixed Economy of Visible Patrols in England and Wales*, Bristol: The Policy Press.

DfES (Department for Education and Skills) (2003) *Every Child Matters*, Cm 5860, London: The Stationery Office.

Farrall, S., Bannister, J., Ditton, J. and Gilchrist, E. (2000) 'Social psychology and the fear of crime', *British Journal of Criminology*, 40(3), pp 399-413.

Flint, J., Atkinson, R. and Scott, S. (2003) *A Report on the Consultation Responses to Putting Our Communities First: A Strategy for Tackling Anti-social Behaviour*, Edinburgh: Scottish Executive.

GfK NOP (2007) *Reflections on Childhood*, London: GfK (www.childrenssociety.org.uk/NR/rdonlyres/DA92712B-5C3F-47C2-87E6-51B8F0C11FFE/0/ReflectionsonChildhoodFriendship.pdf).

Hillman, M., Adams, J. and Whitelegg, J. (1991) *One False Move: A Study of Children's Independent Mobility*, London: Policy Studies Institute.

Home Office (2003) *Respect and Responsibility – Taking a Stand Against Anti-Social Behaviour*, Cm 5778, London: Home Office.

Home Office (2004) *Defining and Measuring Anti-Social Behaviour*, London: Home Office.

Home Office (2005) *Use of Dispersal Powers*, London: Home Office, www.respect.gov.uk/

Home Office (2006a) *Respect Action Plan*, London: Home Office.

Home Office (2006b) *Strengthening Powers to Tackle Anti-Social Behaviour*, Consultation Paper, London: Home Office.

Home Office (2006c) *Respect and Dispersal Powers*, London: Home Office.

Home Office (2007a) *Tools and Powers to Tackle Anti-Social Behaviour*, London: Home Office.

Home Office (2007b) *Strengthening Powers to Tackle Anti-Social Behaviour: Summary of Responses to a Home Office Consultation Paper*, London: Home Office.

House of Commons (2001) *The Criminal Justice and Police Bill: Bill 31 of 2000-2001*, Research Paper, London: House of Commons.

House of Commons Committee of Public Accounts (2007) *Tackling Anti-Social Behaviour*, London: The Stationery Office.

Innes, M. (2004) 'Signal crimes and signal disorder', *British Journal of Sociology*, 55(3), pp 335-55.

Ipsos Mori (2007) *Anti-Social Behaviour – 1000 Practitioner Voices*, available at: www.respect.gov.uk/

Isal, S. (2006) *Equal Respect: ASBOs and Race Equality*, London: The Runnymede Trust.

Jamieson, J., McIvor, G. and Murray, C. (1999) *Understanding Offending Among Young People*, Edinburgh: HMSO.

Kilbrandon Committee (1964) *Report on Children and Young Persons, Scotland*, Edinburgh: HMSO.

Kinsey, R., Lea, J. and Young, J. (1985) *Losing the Fight Against Crime*, Oxford: Blackwell.

Klein, M. (1986) 'Labelling theory and delinquency policy: an empirical test', *Criminal Justice and Behavior*, 13, pp 47-79.

McAra, L. (2005) 'Modelling penal transformation', *Punishment & Society*, 7(3), pp 277-302.

McAra, L. and McVie, S. (2005) 'The usual suspects? Street-life, young people and the police', *Criminal Justice*, 5(1), pp 5-36.

Millie, A., Jacobson, J., McDonald, E. and Hough, M. (2005) *Anti-social Behaviour Strategies: Finding a Balance*, Bristol: The Policy Press.

Morgan, R. (2007) 'Youth justice: a better way forward?', *RSA Journal*, June, available at: www.rsa.org.uk/journal/article.asp?articleID=1059

NAO (National Audit Office) (2006) *The Home Office: Tackling Anti-Social Behaviour*, London: NAO.

Nicholas, S., Kershaw, C. and Walker, A. (2007) *Crime in England and Wales 2006/7*, London: Home Office.

Pearson, G. (1982) *Hooligans: A History of Respectable Fears*, Basingstoke: Macmillan.

Quinton, P., Bland, N. and Miller, J. (2000) *Police Stops, Decision-Making and Practice*, London: Home Office.

Sampson, R.J. and Raudenbush, S.W. (2004) 'Seeing disorder: neighbourhood stigma and the social construction of "broken windows"', *Social Psychology Quarterly*, 67(4), pp 319-42.

Sherman, L., Gottfredson, D., MacKenzie, D., Eck, J., Reuter, P. and Bushway, S. (1997) *Preventing Crime: What Works, What Doesn't, What's Promising*, Washington, DC: National Institute of Justice.

Skogan, W. (2006) 'Asymmetry in the impact of encounters with the police', *Policing and Society*, 16(2), pp 99-126.

Sunshine, J. and Tyler, T. (2003) 'The role of procedural justice and legitimacy in shaping public support for policing', *Law & Society Review*, 37, pp 513-48.

UNICEF (2007) *Child Poverty in Perspective: An Overview of Child Well-Being in Rich Countries*, Florence: UNICEF.

Wheway, R. (2005) *Urban Myths about Children's Playgrounds*, London: Child Action Prevention Trust.

Wilson, D., Sharp, C. and Patterson, A. (2006) *Young People and Crime*, London: Home Office.

YJB (Youth Justice Board) (2006) *Anti-Social Behaviour Orders*, London: YJB.